Conversations about Time

This book presents a conversation between two prominent archaeologists who have been exploring the concept of time in their discipline for several decades. It is a discussion on key issues of time in archaeology filtered through their unique perspectives, which sometimes meet and at other times, clash.

Key features include discussions on the nature of change and time in the archaeological record, the relation between the present and past, the connection between time and the goals of archaeology and the relevance of the Anthropocene to disciplinary practice. Situated in how the authors' own views on the topic of time have developed over their careers, the conversation offers an intimate and personal insight into how two leading scholars think and debate a topic of central importance to the discipline.

All archaeologists with an interest in contemporary theory and the topic of time will find this book of relevance. Also the student who wants a front-row seat onto a live debate on this topic will find it an invaluable complement to the more traditional textbook.

Gavin Lucas is Professor of Archaeology at the University of Iceland. His main research interests lie in archaeological method and theory and the archaeology of the modern world. His most recent books include *Writing the Past* (2019) and *Making Time* (2021), both also published by Routledge.

Laurent Olivier is Chief Curator of the Celtic and Gallic Department of the National Museum of Archaeology at Saint-Germain-en-Laye, France. His main research interests are in archaeological history and theory and Iron Age archaeology. His most recent books include *Le Pays des Celtes: mémoires de la Gaule* (2018) and *César contre Vercingétorix* (2019).

Conversations about Time

Gavin Lucas and Laurent Olivier

Routledge
Taylor & Francis Group

LONDON AND NEW YORK

First published 2022
by Routledge
2 Park Square, Milton Park, Abingdon, Oxon OX14 4RN

and by Routledge
605 Third Avenue, New York, NY 10158

Routledge is an imprint of the Taylor & Francis Group, an informa business

British Library Cataloguing-in-Publication Data
A catalogue record for this book is available from the British Library

Library of Congress Cataloging-in-Publication Data
Names: Lucas, Gavin, 1965- author. | Olivier, Laurent, 1958- author.
Title: Conversations about time / Gavin Lucas and Laurent Olivier.
Description: Abingdon, Oxon ; New York, NY : Routledge, 2022. | Includes bibliographical references and index.
Identifiers: LCCN 2021015433 (print) | LCCN 2021015434 (ebook) | ISBN 9781032024868 (hbk) | ISBN 9781032024950 (pbk) | ISBN 9781003183600 (ebk)
Subjects: LCSH: Archaeology--Methodology. | Time--Philosophy. | Archaeology--Philosophy. | Lucas, Gavin, 1965---Interviews. | Olivier, Laurent, 1958---Interviews.
Classification: LCC CC75.7 .L834 2022 (print) | LCC CC75.7 (ebook) | DDC 930.101--dc23
LC record available at https://lccn.loc.gov/2021015433
LC ebook record available at https://lccn.loc.gov/2021015434

ISBN: 978-1-032-02486-8 (hbk)
ISBN: 978-1-032-02495-0 (pbk)
ISBN: 978-1-003-18360-0 (ebk)

DOI: 10.4324/9781003183600

Typeset in Times New Roman
by MPS Limited, Dehradun

Contents

Figures

Tables

Prologue

The writing of this book was something of an accident, yet perhaps also inevitable. One of us (Gavin) had just finished a draft of a new book about time in archaeology[1] and had asked the other (Laurent) if he would be willing to read it over and offer some useful commentary and critique before publication. This he kindly did but rather than send an annotated file back, Laurent sent his thoughts in a series of emails to which Gavin would occasionally respond. In the course of this exchange, a discussion emerged exploring some of the differences of our positions and as Laurent was finishing Gavin's manuscript, he suggested that maybe we should develop this exchange into an extended conversation: 'So, perhaps we should think about writing a book together as a dialogue about time ... to discuss what we know and what we don't, how we approach things ... It could be a book ... showing how we think, how we doubt ...'. That was at the beginning of September 2020. Three months later, we had written around 40,000 words of conversation which forms the basis of this book.

There is no doubt the current situation which the world finds itself in over the period this book was written was conducive to this process. The coronavirus pandemic that hit us at the beginning of 2020 changed our lives and is still ongoing as we write this at the beginning of 2021; it is hard to predict what long-term impact it will have. But in the midst of it, many of us have found that collaborative writing – which was always an activity that web-based and online platforms were supposed to be ideal for promoting – became an opportunity to good to miss. It is ironic that it took a situation which locked us into our home countries, even our homes, to bring us finally together. Because as we later relate in our conversation, we have known each other since the early 1990s when we were both doctoral students at Cambridge. Both of us were working on the topic of time and although we paid attention to each other's work, we have never collaborated until now.

Yet perhaps such collaboration was inevitable. In 2014, Laurent co-hosted a workshop in Metz in France and invited Gavin to partici-pate.[2] Three years later, Gavin invited Laurent to Reykjavík in Iceland as a guest lecturer at a PhD seminar. Such occasions, though rare, enabled us to meet and exchange ideas, get a better sense of what the other was doing and thinking. It was clear to both of us that we were circling around similar questions but often from very different angles and positions. We also came from very different intellectual back-grounds; even though we both studied at Cambridge, by this time much of our intellectual framework had been long established and the differences between us often proved frustrating, leading us to misread or not fully understand what the other was saying.

Possibly it was this frustration as much as the recognition of sharing the same matters of concern that led us to the point of starting this dialogue. Rather than carry on writing separate papers and books, we both saw the benefit of engaging in an extended and deep conversation which could untangle some of the knots of frustration and enable us to explore together questions that bothered both of us. Indeed, as much as it was a chance to talk about time, it was also an opportunity to resuscitate an old genre of scientific writing: epistolary correspon-dence. That early publications of archaeological findings often took the form of a letter is well known,[3] but in many ways, these published texts are an indication of a much wider practice of scholarly corre-spondence that goes back to the 17th century and earlier. In an age before planes and trains, when long-distance travel was still a major commitment, exchanging ideas with colleagues largely took place through letter-writing. Living amidst a global pandemic, we find ourselves in a similar situation today in the 21st century – although now, the speed at which such correspondence takes place tempers such comparison. The fact that we can complete such a correspondence in three months which in the 17th century, may have taken three years, alerts us to the fact that time was not only our topic of conversation, it also structures the nature of that conversation.

Dialogues are not new to archaeology and e-mails have certainly facilitated their production, whether this is acknowledged or not. The dialogic format has also been promoted as an important alternative to the traditional scholarly paper.[4] But while the inspiration for such a format is often attributed to Plato's Socratic dialogues and its med-ieval imitators, our role model has been the letter-writing of the new science of natural philosophy that emerged in 17th century Europe. Indeed, the fact that this book was written, not spoken, that it took the form of an epistolary correspondence through email, is an important quality. Unlike dialogue, letter-writing allows one to pause and reflect, to take time to compose an answer; despite the speed of emails over traditional post, there is still a shared temporality in composition. And even if email letters still accelerate this process relative to hand-written correspondence, it is important to acknowledge that this is still a written conversation, not a transcript of a spoken one. Moreover, it was also a deliberate decision to write this conversation through email rather than through online multi-user word processing formats like Google Docs, as it preserved something of the letter-writing spirit.

For us, this has been a very exciting and stimulating exercise, continuously bringing new insights, discovering that we were sometimes much closer in our thinking than we thought, but then at other times, far apart. The process has helped us understand each other's approach in a deeper manner and in so doing, understand ourselves better. Especially when talking with a colleague from a different cultural and intellectual background, one becomes more aware of the peculiarities of one's own position – but also the unacknowledged prejudices one has towards others. Moreover, such differences often blinded us to the fact that we were ultimately addressing the same issues, the same concerns and often making the same observations but simply expressing them in different terms. The desire to understand what the other is saying is important here; even in such close engagements as this, there is always the danger one strives to simply proselytize, preach, proclaim one's own position. Stating your position is important but so is listening. At the end of the day, the primary motivation for this conversation was to listen and learn from each other. After all, our individual positions are clearly staked out in other publications.

It is also for this reason that we regard this conversation as worthy of publication; although beneficial for us, we believe and hope the reader will also get some stimulation from reading this. For we address issues which concern the whole discipline and we do so in a manner which ideally, shows how important debate and discussion is to working through such issues. There are more than enough books out there which give us summaries of concepts and issues, which present an author's own particular take on a subject. But archaeology, like any discipline, is a communal and social activity and especially when it comes to issues of theoretical concern, conversation is surely one of the most appropriate genres to adopt. It shows archaeological thinking as alive, as dynamic, as a process, something one often only observes at conferences or seminars. At the end of the day, we hope our readers will get as much pleasure from reading this as we did in writing it.

The following conversations all took place through email but by cumulatively adding to a document. In all, we exchanged this document 60 times and although it has undergone some minor editing, what you will read is more or less what we wrote to each other. We divided the conversations into five chapters but otherwise retained the temporal sequence of our exchanges. The manuscript was then reviewed by two anonymous referees who provided important, critical distance; it is hard to make changes to a dialogue after it has been written, much harder than a regular text and the reviewers acknowledged this. However, we wanted to take on board some of their comments so we added a final, supplemental dialogue at the end (chapter 6), which uses these reviews as a basis for responding to some of the issues we imagined some of our readers might want to know more about – especially issues which we did not address in the main conversation.

So what should the reader expect? This is not an introduction to theoretical debate around time in archaeology; for that, there are other books and texts available, including one written by one of us.[5] We don't survey 'the state of the art' and some readers will probably be disappointed by omissions or uneven coverage. For readers less familiar with our works and for students, this may be off-putting. And yet because of the conversational and personal style in which this is written, we feel that even a reader with little familiarity with our positions should be able to follow the dialogue. We situate the topics and problems we discuss within very concrete contexts and to help the reader, we provide short outlines at the head of each chapter. These are part traditional abstracts/summaries, part guides to reading.

The first two chapters chart the chronological development of our thinking, starting at Cambridge where we first met while doing our doctoral research in the 1990s and then how our work developed thereafter. The last three chapters go on to explore various issues around time that have occupied us since and are roughly organized around three concepts: the past, present and future. The final chapter, as already mentioned, provides a short attempt to anticipate readers misgivings about major omissions in the previous chapters; it is inevitably truncated and selective but hopefully it at least acknowledges some of the gaps in our main discussion. Rather than offer any further summary of what is discussed in these chapters, we invite the reader to simply start reading; after all, the point lies in the process. At the end of this book however, we offer some general reflections on the conversation and try and draw out the key points that were discussed, especially in relation to where we agree and disagree, concluding with a joint proposition – or provocation about time and archaeology.

Bon appétit.

Gavin Lucas and Laurent Olivier,
Reykjavík and Saint-Germain-en-Laye,
13.40 and 15.40, 23rd February 2021

Notes

1. G. Lucas, *Making Time. The Archaeology of Time Revisited* (Routledge: London, 2021).
2. J.-M. Blaising, J. Driessen, J.-P. Legendre and L. Olivier, *Clashes of Time. The Contemporary Past as a Challenge for Archaeology* (Louvain-la-Neuve: Presses universitaires de Louvain, 2017).
3. I. Hodder, 'Writing Archaeology: site reports in context', *Antiquity* 63 (1989): 268–274.
4. R. Joyce, *The Languages of Archaeology. Dialogue, Narrative and Writing* (Oxford: Blackwell Publishers, 2002).
5. G. Lucas, *The Archaeology of Time* (London and New York: Routledge, 2005).

Bibliography

Blaising, J.-M., J. Driessen, J.-P. Legendre, and L. Olivier. *Clashes of Time. The Contemporary Past as a Challenge for Archaeology.* Louvain-la-Neuve: Presses universitaires de Louvain, 2017.
Hodder, I. 'Writing archaeology: site reports in context', *Antiquity* 63 (1989): 268–274.
Joyce, R. *The Languages of Archaeology. Dialogue, Narrative and Writing.* Oxford: Blackwell Publishers, 2002.
Lucas, G. *The Archaeology of Time.* London and New York: Routledge, 2005.
Lucas, G. *Making Time. The Archaeology of Time Revisited.* Routledge: London, 2021.

1   In the beginning

Archaeology has always had a problem with time. At its very core, dating is a fundamental part of what we do and before the advent of scientific techniques like C14, archaeologists relied heavily on methods such as stratigraphy, typology and seriation. In this chapter, we talk about our earliest research on time as part of our doctoral studies, where both of us dealt with problems around the latter two methods, typology and seriation. Although scientific methods of dating dominate today, the legacy of typology and seriation is still strong in the way they subtly inform our perception of time and change in the archaeological record. We expect change to be sequential, linear and regular. What we found through experimental work on modern, well-dated objects is that artefacts did not in fact obey the temporal assumptions and principles which guided the traditional methods of typological progression or seriation. That time looked very different from an artefact's point of view. These empirical observations found theoretical support in other fields; for Laurent, the work of Freud on memory was the key, while for Gavin, it was the philosopher Husserl and phenomenological studies of time consciousness that were most productive. For both of us though, this was the beginning of a journey that drew us deeper and deeper into the complexities of time in archaeology.

Gavin: Both of us have written a lot about time in archaeology and is a topic we share a deep interest in. Moreover, despite knowing each other now for more than a quarter of a century, we have never really had an opportunity to explore this mutual interest. Perhaps it is only fitting to begin at the beginning. *How and why did you get interested in time?*

Laurent: Do you remember? We met at Cambridge in the 90's, when we were writing our PhD's. I was a bit older than the other guys, as I had already been working as a professional archaeologist in France for nearly ten years. I had come to Cambridge because I was attracted by the anthropological and sociological perspective brought by Anglo-American research on archaeology – something which was completely lacking at that time in French research, at least in my field: Iron Age archaeology.

So I went to Cambridge, thinking of writing a piece of research about the mortuary practices of Celtic cultures in Eastern France in the last millennium BC.[1] But very soon, I realized that the key question that

DOI: 10.4324/9781003183600-1

had to be solved first wasn't how to interpret archaeological evidence; I mean how to use material remains to understand past practices and past beliefs or past cultural representations. It was time. Not time in general, not time abstractly; but time in the archaeological record: that is to say, how time is recorded within archaeological matter.

It was obvious, for instance, that there were different chronological dynamics at work within my archaeological data: clearly, the traditions of building graves and funerary monuments weren't moving at the same speed as those attached to the placing of grave goods as offerings, and similar discrepancies were also visible according to differences among the deceased: men and women, adults and children, rich and poor people ... And perhaps more worrying, the flow of time wasn't running at the same pace within the different periods of time reconstructed by archaeology: sometimes it was very slow, or very quick on the contrary; sometimes it was running over very long periods of time, and then suddenly very short ones. I was facing a complete mess: how to put together any coherent narrative about the past in this situation?

So I began to realize that there was a problem with time in archaeology. Because time was differently recorded according to the various ways that immaterial practices were materially translated in the archaeological record, I suspected that the problem lay in this material recording. In other words, I began to understand that I had to think of time as attached to matter. As something relative – being related to materiality – and not as an absolute measurement, independent of everything.

Put like that, it sounds rather abstract. To get a clearer idea of what was going on, I constructed an experiment. What would happen if, for instance, we would try to date contemporary artefacts such as a series of miner's lamps – already perfectly dated to within a year and distributed over nearly two centuries – according to archaeological methods of dating, specifically seriation? To put it otherwise, what would happen if we would project these material productions into a perfect mathematical linear time, in which time is measured by uninterrupted change? Would it disturb the ordering of 'real time', which was marked by the dates of production of these artefacts? In other words, would archaeological matter behave in its own way, independently of this absolute and abstract time of clocks?

Of course it did. It even did so spectacularly. Each part of these technical objects was travelling time at its own speed, sometimes alone, sometimes in synchrony with some of the others. Some of them are like shooting stars, suddenly expanding and then disappearing, others are just dull throughout their life, some die and then come back as if nothing had happened in the interim. Change is sometimes in advance and sometimes very late: it depends on what you are looking at. Therefore, time doesn't follow a peculiar direction: things just happen in the way they do, if I can put it like this. Above all, there is no absolute 'real time' in the archaeological record; it is just as simple as that. And what this means for archaeology is huge. So this was the beginning, in fact. I must say that it was unexpected: I just found a thread and, as I was searching, I pulled on it and it came.

Gavin: Like you I was working on time for my PhD only how I came to it was rather different. After my undergraduate studies, I too went into commercial archaeology but only for a short period – a year or two, before starting my doctoral studies. When I started my PhD, I had a topic all prepared: the role of ethnographic analogy. It had fascinated me as an undergraduate, perhaps because I had a North American archaeologist teach me theory (Ann Stahl), but more generally, I always knew that theoretical archaeology was going to be a core interest. Ever since I started working on excavations since the age of 16, I was also an avid reader of philosophy and these twin passions have more or less driven my career ever since. Bringing them together through theoretical archaeology was simply inevitable so taking a theoretical topic for my PhD was an obvious choice. It is perhaps also why when my supervisor Ian Hodder suggested switching my topic from analogy to time, I went along without much protest. The thrill was in grappling with conceptual problems and time served just as well as analogy.

Next to your 'conversion' to time, mine probably sounds terribly shallow and superficial. But maybe the initial reasons aren't as important as what you go on to do with the choices you have made. My interest in time during the PhD was ironically though, somewhat removed from excavation and the concerns you had; I was more caught up with questions of material form, design, typology and how time in archaeology intersected with these issues. Possibly this was due to the fact that I developed a specialism in Romano-British ceramics prior to starting my PhD, not from taking courses but working through assemblages. During my doctoral studies, I supplemented my income by analyzing and writing up reports on pottery assemblages for commercial projects, and although I also occasionally did a bit of digging as well, it was probably working on artefact assemblages that formed my primary bridge to the more theoretical work of my PhD. And so we come to the article I wrote on clocks.[2] One of the wonderful things my supervisor made me do was write up some experimental papers on modern objects to explore the issues I was interested in. I remember writing about the changing design of pistols and umbrellas, but it was the one on clocks that I ended up publishing, probably because it seemed so apt. After all, my key interest was in the relation of time to form. Obviously biological evolution was always important here but so was art history, especially the work of Kubler who was a student of Focillon[3] – someone who you recently pointed out to me. But at the heart of this work I came to very similar conclusions as you. Archaeology typically portrayed typological development in terms of an evolution of types, one replacing the other, whereas what I found studying the design of umbrellas, pistols and clocks is that they didn't change like this. What I found was that some elements would stay the same, others would change and that different elements had different tempos or rates of change. In fact it was more interesting to break form or design down into individual elements and trace their trajectories rather than think in terms of typological progression. Once you do this, you can start to ask far more specific questions about how form changes, why some elements change at the same time and others not, why some change at faster rates than others and so on. In other words, studying the temporality of design or form of objects threw up all the same issues that you seem to have faced with your site and its multiple temporalities.

Laurent: It is amazing to see how close and how far away from each other we were at that time. We were, and we still are, close, since, like you, I began working on excavations when I was 15. And, like you, I passionately discovered philosophy when I was 17, I guess – and more particularly the field of the history of ideas, thanks to Michel Foucault's work. And it is surprising to me to discover how close we were working at Cambridge at that time on different subjects, with different approaches, coming from different intellectual backgrounds – but also how isolated we were, each of us trying to make sense of his own stuff.

So what did you see, studying these modern things? How would you explain the relation of time and form, which was your concern?

Gavin: This throws up an interesting issue. In purely formal or design terms, there is no difference between Roman pottery and clocks. We can study both and look at how technology, materials, design intertwine. But in temporal terms there is an important difference. With modern objects like clocks we often have better information on dates as with your miner's lamps so we can start with time under control, so to speak. Conventionally with archaeological objects, the situation is not like this – in fact it is the opposite: you are often using form or design to elicit chronology, that is often your goal, not your starting point. The advantage of using modern objects then is you can re-examine time without worrying about chronology. Of course not all modern objects are necessarily that easy to date and some older ones do come with dates – here I am thinking for example of Deetz and Dethlefsen's famous analysis of New England gravestones to demonstrate popularity curves of design.[4] This study is often mistakenly given as an example of seriation, but in fact it is nothing of the sort; seriation has no dates, rather you are using the assumption of popularity curves to chronologically order pottery for example. Again, time is your goal, not your starting point.

Now this difference is important and also liberating. Because if you have dated objects already, then you can start to explore the relation between time and form in a different way. And what I tried to show is how an object – even one with a single date stamp – was actually always a composite of the old and the new. It has temporal layers, some of these layers stretched back very far, some were more recent. In a way, I was trying to stratify design and form, but the superposition of strata was not like deposits in the ground but more like different time-lines bundled together, imbricated or overlapping. I think one of my main goals here was to make us think about the relation of time to typology in a different way. Instead of seeing types succeeding one and another or even over-lapping in popularity curves as with the gravestone study of Deetz, I wanted to argue that a type itself was a composite of overlapping layers or elements. Once we see types as stratified like this, we can then take this method and apply it to archaeological objects and focus on their tem-poral layers rather than types – which is what I tried to do with my PhD material, which dealt with later prehistory of northern England.[5]

I am not sure I was that successful however! Indeed, I think you were taking a far more sophisticated approach to time than I was back then by the sounds of things. And yet you are right – we were both very close in some ways in the work we were doing yet strangely working in isolation. I have recently reflected on this; Cambridge at this time was a hotbed of research on time, not just us but others were there in the 1990s like James McGlade, Tim Murray and Geoff Bailey. Possibly you interacted more with them than I did, but for some reason I really did not make use of this environment; I was stuck in my own corner of postprocessualism, pursuing my own train of thought. It is only many years later I really came to appreciate the work of these archaeologists and indeed yours.

But perhaps you can tell me more of your experiments, the ones with the miner's lamps. Like my clocks they had date stamps; but what did you find when you applied an archaeological approach to them? What happened?

Laurent: I am truly flabbergasted by what you are telling me. We were not only studying the same sort of things – modern objects – but we were seeing the same kinds of processes on artefacts when they were projected in 'real time', by which I mean our common time of clocks. I saw in my miner's lamps exactly what you saw in your clocks. As you say, finding time wasn't the goal, since 'real time' was already there, in the accurate dating of the objects which was already known. And yes, it was liberating! So, I used this advantage to test our conventional methods of 'relative dating', based on seriations. At that time, I had it in mind to check which statistical method would be the most efficient to capture 'real time', by applying different kinds of seriation to my set of hundreds of miner's lamps. My (stupid) plan was to get to this point: 'Look, I have tested all of these, and I can tell you that the best seriation is this one, which I then applied to my Iron Age archaeological dataset'.

It was foolish because, in fact, none of the methods really worked. The best ones were the most vague and inaccurate in their results, those we would usually consider as the least effective of all. But I began to understand why it didn't work. As you pointed out, each artefact, each material creation, is a composite of the old and the new. It is a stratified composition indeed, our layers being here typological details in the shape of your clocks, or technical pieces in my miner's lamps. But, as with any site, the deposit of these 'layers' is not regular: it isn't the same sequence everywhere, on every object, at the same time. Quite often, the 'new' comes in advance. Most of the time, this is just a detail invented or added somewhere. It eventually becomes 'popular' later on, but not necessarily. Sometimes it appears and then disappears.

So what do seriations do in this case? They group together the same attributes; they sort what looks alike and push away what doesn't. They crush these scattered attributes related to the early emergence of the 'new' together with the mass of those belonging to the later 'usual'. This is the reason why so often you get this 'accordion effect' in archaeological chronologies: a first typo-chronological period which is quite long and relatively empty – in terms of types and typological attributes – then suddenly a short one, quite full, and then again a long and boring sequence... And this is also the reason why we have so many 'transition periods' in archaeology: they are basically a mixture of the old and the new which cannot be sorted. All of that never existed in 'real time'; all of that is just a side-effect of our conventional methods to date the past.

Gavin: This is really interesting. I know exactly what you are talking about with this accordion effect – but I have always assumed it somehow reflects something about how innovations actually develop. This is what you hear also in technology stories and I have also heard the same ideas applied to Darwinian evolution with new species. That whenever you get something new, there is a flood of variations and experiments, but eventually, most of these die out and only one or two survive to become the norm. But what you seem to be saying is that this is simply an effect of our chronological methods and does not really capture the way things develop.

Laurent: This general process you are describing is indeed what was happening with my miner's lamps, within the real course of time. What I am talking about here is what seriations do to the chronological ordering of these individuals in 'real time', when they try to order them under their own ideal linear time. The trouble begins here. I mean that these statistical methods cut this constant flow of the appearance and disappearance of attributes, creating artificial typo-chronological groups. Of course, you can see that only when you are privileged enough to be able to compare the 'real time' of what happened with the 'artificial time' of what has been statistically reconstructed.

The seriations we commonly use in archaeology are based on the search for the first appearance of attributes. Within the combinations of criteria we offer them, they look for what seems to come first, then second and so forth... and they rearrange the matrix in order to get a nice diagonal effect, which is supposed to translate into a movement across time. To put it in another way, these seriations are based on the principle that regular and uninterrupted change may be exploited as a direct measurement of time.

That's fair enough, but in doing so, these methods are in fact distorting the order that the artefacts had in 'real time'. Seriations cannot deal with the fact that there is often a period of latency between the very first appearance of early attributes – which suddenly pop up somewhere – and their later adoption by most of the population. So the method groups together all the individuals bearing these peculiar attributes, no matter what their respective position is in 'real time'.

And there is a symmetrical problem when change is slowing down or just not happening anymore. It usually happens when types become 'popular' or 'successful': they are standardized. For seriation, which is blindly looking for repeated changes, time has just stopped moving. Seriations had no way to distinguish, for instance, these miner's lamps produced in Western Europe in the 1880's from those made in Poland in the 1970's, since they are basically alike.

So when you look at the speed and intensity of these sequences of change, projecting these trajectories expressed by 'real time' onto the ideal linear time of 'artificial time', you observe a strange phenomenon: this archaeological 'real time' – the time of objects, as it has happened – is snaking up and down along the ideal axis of pure linear time. The initial periods of innovation are clearly 'in advance' of regular time – they are lying in its future – while those of standardization are late, being in the past of what should be the present situation if time was regular. This is, I believe, the expression of the 'accordion effect' you were talking about (Figure 1.1).

But here something quite disturbing is occurring: 'real time', the time of things that have actually happened, is not the 'ideal time', the irreversible time of clocks on which any chronology is based. In other words, dates and dating belong to different universes, which are irreconcilable. This is bad news for archaeology, but this is also very bad news for our understanding of time in archaeology: common time (the time of chronology) cannot deal with the 'real time' of the artefacts, which should correlate with the true 'archaeological time'.

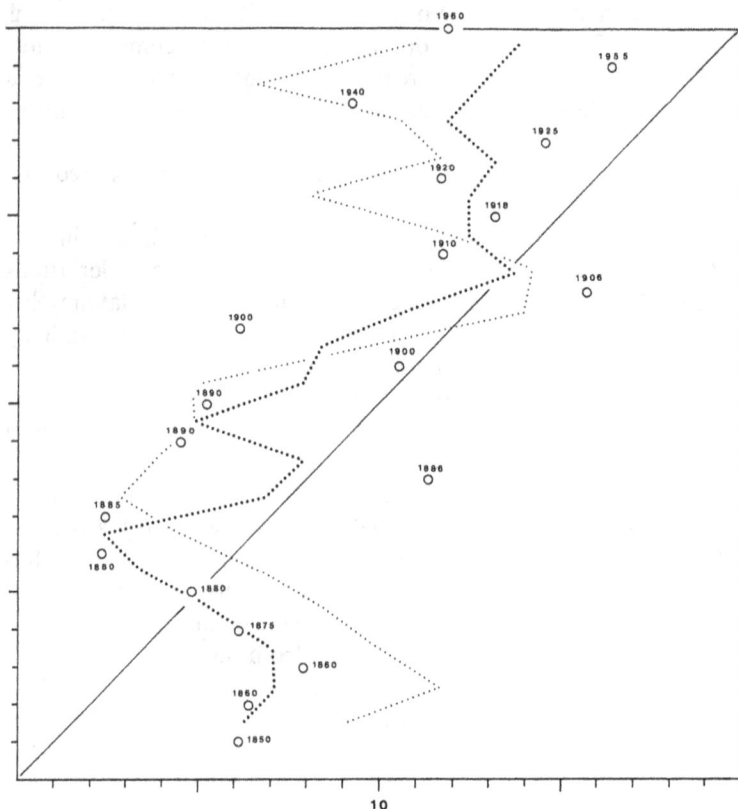

Figure 1.1 Gradient Vector Analysis on which you see the internal time of the
miner's lamps 'snaking' up and down around the 'ideal linear time'
(after Olivier 1994).

Gavin: This is a really important point and I think this figure you
show of the 'lamp time' snaking around chronological time is
incredible. Every archaeologist needs to see it as it gives us an
immediate and visual kick up the backside. What it shows is
that change is not regular, but sometimes ahead of itself
(spurts of innovation as when the line snakes to the right of
the straight vector), sometimes holding back (a conservatism
that keeps the line to the left). More crucially, it shows how
the in-built assumptions about regular change behind
seriation need to be corrected.

This must have been a great discovery for your research?

Laurent: To tell you the truth, this was nice but not very helpful with regard to what I was looking for in order to write my PhD ... I came to realize that I had deeply failed in my previous excavation projects. You said you were stuck in your own corner of postprocessualism and so was I in my own world. At that time, we had a living God, who reigned over French prehistory. His name was André Leroi-Gourhan. People around him used to call this new prophet '*le patron*' – the boss. He was in a sense a postprocessualist in his own way, since he completely changed the way we practiced and interpreted prehistoric archaeology in the 1970s. To put it crudely, before him prehistoric archaeology was a matter of stratigraphy and archaeological sequences observed in caves and rock shelters; it was based on a vertical approach of the past, so to speak. Leroi-Gourhan made it horizontal: he developed meticulous stripping of '*prehistoric floors*', reconstructing the gestures, practices and habits of the people who lived there from what humble remains they had left on the ground.[6] His approach was truly revolutionary: such an '*ethnographic excavation*' was striving to read, for the very first time and on very basic archaeological evidence, how people had been behaving, what they had done and maybe what they had thought and felt[7].

I was one of his believers. I thought that I could do the same for other periods of the past such as Iron Age Celtic archaeology. On burial mounds, for instance. As with prehistoric floors, people had been performing ceremonies around the graves of their people, they had made offerings, surely they had followed some rituals with those material products that had been deposited in the ground. Then, they had sealed these 'funerary floors' with huge piles of soil or stones, over hundreds, sometimes thousands of square meters. If I could excavate this as carefully as Leroi-Gourhan's team did at Pincevent,[8] then I could develop a far more interesting Iron Age archaeology: an archaeology focused on people rather on objects.

This was a brilliant plan, but the trouble was that I never found any of those 'funerary floors'. I excavated dozens of mounds and what I got wasn't what I had expected. There was no floor at all, but sometimes a vague horizon, about 10 cm thick, containing tiny, scattered pieces of pottery, in some places flint flakes or eroded fragments of grindstones... How to be sure this was related to the building of the burial mound, and, if it was really the case, how to be sure that all these remains were the result of the same sequence of events, associated with the burial of the dead? And what about those unidentifiable sherds, the ordinary pieces of stone; were they there already when the Iron Age people came, centuries perhaps millennia later?

I was alarmed and in fact worried; I was realizing how mad I had been to accept Sander Van der Leeuw's proposal to come to Cambridge to write a PhD under his supervision. The more I was trying to fix this mess with time in my archaeological data, the worse it got... You are right, looking back to the 1990s, Cambridge was the place where several of us were already exploring new perspectives on time. But in my case, it was with anguish and loneliness; we were all in our corners, with our own concerns, our own attempts, our own academic backgrounds. In fact, I must say that I was trying to fix a problem with time in order to do something very conventional: reconstructing the past as it was, insofar as I thought it was possible to reach it at least. James McGlade was using non-linear mathematics for quite the same purpose: reconstructing, in much more detail, the life of the agro-pastoral communities of Bronze Age Wessex.[9] I realize now that this tear in time, that we were all encountering, in each of our corners, was some kind of wormhole, opening onto real and new universes, a widening hole in the net of archaeological methods and theories. But we were blind at that time – at least I was.

And what about you, what were your feelings at that time? Were there people who had a strong intellectual influence on you, or helped you to go deeper into time? How did you manage?

Gavin: I was very close to my supervisor Ian Hodder for the first year or 18 months; we had regular meetings and would bat ideas back and forth; he was almost my only intellectual soundboard, though of course I was talking with some of the other PhD students, but mostly those who were also Ian's students. It all sounds very cliquey now, but at time it just seemed natural; I think it was more just a case of Ian's students were the ones I tended to meet. I certainly don't recall this ever being intentional... but maybe that's just how Cambridge was back then. But as I mentioned earlier, there was probably also the 'postprocessual club' aspect to it all.

Anyhow, apart from my discussions with Ian, most of my other influences came from reading. Besides just catching up on postprocessual theory (I had come from an undergraduate degree in London where I received a deep training in processual theory, and postprocessualism was a vague revolution on the horizon – this was the mid-late 1980s), I immersed myself in studies on time by philosophers and anthropologists, with a smattering of other stuff from sociology, technology studies and art history. Philosophically, I was deep into post-structuralism – Derrida especially but apart from a few works, he was not specifically useful for thinking about time. In the end, it was phenomenology and hermeneutics: Levinas but especially Heidegger and Ricoeur, that were my main influences. What is interesting though is how these thinkers took me far away from my studies of clocks and the temporality of form that we have just been discussing. In the end, I was thinking more about the relation between history and narrative than time and form. And I think this shift in some ways came because of my discussions with Hodder who was all into Hayden White at this time.

Laurent: *It would be nice if you could tell me more about what you learnt at that time from philosophy, in relation to your first work on archaeological time through the study of modern objects. Could you elaborate a bit more?*

Gavin: Well, of all the philosophers I was reading at that time, I think without doubt Husserl had the greatest impact, at least in relation to this study of objects. For me, the key problem was about how to mediate continuity and change in a way that did not force them apart into opposites. For example, the traditional approach to time and typology had objects stabilizing as types, which then persisted for a certain period to be replaced by a new type. So you had periods of continuity followed by abrupt moments of change. I wanted to explore ways in which continuity and change could be expressed together, not apart and Husserl provided the best way for me to visualize this. He used the example of a musical note ringing in the air; like Bergson, he wanted to understand how time could incorporate both the idea of a present moment passing, and of the past persisting into the present. How can time both flow and yet we still have sense of past, present and future as distinct temporalities? Although I have grown to appreciate Bergson more in subsequent years, at the time I felt Husserl offered a far more useful way to tackle this, especially for archaeology.[10] He stratified time with his time diagrams, which showed how the present is both a flow (depicted by a line moving forward) and yet as it flows, it leaves ripples in its wake like a wave that remains as ghostly

Past   Present
A   B   C

A'   B'   C'

A"   B"   C"

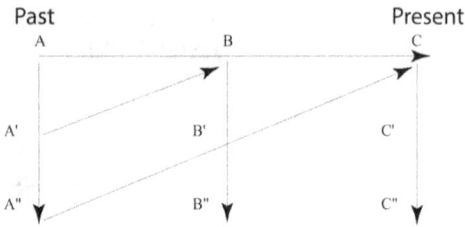

Figure 1.2 Husserl's Diagram of time consciousness (after Lucas 2005, fig. 1.5).

retentions of the past in the present (depicted by both vertical lines descending from the horizontal flow of the present, and as oblique lines rebounding back up to meet the line at a later point than from where they descended) (Figure 1.2):

Basically, what this diagram told me is that to represent continuity and change in the same breath, I need to give time a depth, a stratigraphy; not in the conventional archaeological sense, but rather to show that the time of object design or form is layered and that any change always takes place against continuity and vice versa. So for any one dated object, like your miner's lamp or my clock, we should always think of it almost as a vertical slice or cross section through one of Husserl's time diagrams where it incorporates elements of variously older or more recent traits. This fundamentally was what Kubler was also telling me in his discussion that all art forms comprise a blend of convention and invention, the old and new. It seems to me that when we combine this with your vector analysis of the miner's lamps, it tells us that this combination of invention and convention is never equalized but sometimes you have more of one, sometimes more of the other, creating that snaking line. So with Husserl's time diagrams, I found a way to think about design and form of objects as temporally layered or stratified.

But what about you? Who were your influences?

Laurent: I came to Cambridge thanks to Sander van der Leeuw, who offered to be my PhD supervisor, and Alain Schnapp, who helped me to get a grant from the CNRS (the French National Centre of Scientific Research) to support my university fees. At that time, the CNRS was funding French scholars to study in British universities. Alain had been my professor at the University of Paris-Sorbonne, when I was a Master's student there. My interest in the history of ideas in archaeology comes directly from his teaching.[11] At Cambridge, Sander was living with Anick Coudart, who had been Jean-Paul Demoule's girlfriend for a long time when they began to excavate Early Neolithic settlements in the Aisne Valley. Jean-Paul and Anick had also been teaching archaeology when I was a student, together with a very nice man – who died, unfortunately. His name was Serge Cleuziou and he worked as an archaeologist in Oman. Pierre Lemonnier – who had also been one of Anick's boyfriends – was around too. As an anthropologist, he was working with Maurice Godelier in Papua New Guinea.

Told like this, it looks like a French movie by Claude Sautet ... But this was a small group of friendly people, who were very close to each other and I always maintained contacts with them over the years. I liked them, since they were original, bright and open minded – compared to the 'traditional' archaeologists in the 'provinces' (that is to say everywhere but in Paris) who used to strongly dislike them. They had a good reason for that: these 'Parisians' were taking sides with the Anglo-American 'New archaeologists'. In 1980, they had published a book, simply entitled *Archaeology Today*, which had been a revelation to me:[12] there, I discovered Rathje's *Garbage Project*, the use of Harris matrices and seriations, rank-size analysis and British spatial archaeology, and, of course, the debates which were going on about processual archaeology.

So I came from this intellectual milieu when I moved to Cambridge in the 1990s. There, I talked a lot with Sander van der Leeuw, especially about innovation and the environment, Michael Shanks about photography and memory and James McGlade about many things but above all history... And like you I read. I read as much as I could, spending all my time at the Haddon and University libraries. I tried to read all that I hadn't read and I should know. The 'Classics' of course: Binford, Renfrew, Clarke, Hodder ... The archaeology of death and social archaeology, necessarily: Chapman, Rowlands, Bintliff ... But more and more people who had been working on the nature of the archaeological record; I mean what it records and how it does it: Binford again, William Rathje, Michael Schiffer[13]...

Because I was moving away from Leroi-Gourhan's methodological influence – as I had realized, as François Bordes put it, that prehistoric floors were indeed 'a matter of faith'[14] – I didn't read much of the postprocessualists. I had the feeling that approaching the archaeological evidence in that way was a bit like chasing the rainbow: you see it, you think you can catch it; but when you move towards it, it steps back. But I was not going back to processualism either; I was looking for another way, a different approach that would grasp the specificity of the archaeological record.

Gavin: French archaeologists seem as incestuous as British ones! But it does sound like we both came to Cambridge with a great appetite and hunger to read and find out what was happening in archaeology at this time. But you have talked a lot about archaeological influences; what about other ones, philosophical ones perhaps? I think British academics have always been a bit envious of the way philosophy in France is more integrated into general intellectual life; but at the same time, it always surprised me how little French archaeologists seem to cite or reference philosophers whereas in Britain, it almost became *de rigueur* in the 1980s and 1990s.

So how did philosophy fit into your archaeology at this time? Or did it?

Laurent: It is as if you and I were digging a tunnel from opposite sides of the same mountain: in your British gallery, you were reading philosophical works in order to provide you with some theoretical framework allowing you to think through your archaeological data; while, on my French side, I was trying to extract this framework first from my archaeological stuff, in order to confront it then go to the works of those thinkers that would explain its structure and behavior best. That's definitely two different intellectual perspectives and this is the reason why it is sometimes so difficult to understand each other from the opposite sides of the Channel.

So clearly you were far in advance on me! I came to philosophy at the very end of my Cambridge years, looking at Bergson of course, and his *Matter and Memory*, but also the German phenomenologists, such as Husserl and the late Heidegger. So basically the same people that you read. But here, at this point of our exchange, I have to explain how I came to these people we had in common, following a path which – I am just realizing that today – was crossing your own.

Sarah Tarlow and Brian Boyd were running the *Archaeological Review from Cambridge*, the little student journal we had at Downing Street.[15] They were preparing a special issue on the archaeology of death and, as I was working on this topic, they asked me to contribute a paper. We agreed that a case study would be more concrete than a digest of general reflections. So I chose to present the German Hochdorf grave, a 'princely' burial of the late 6th century BC, which had been excellently excavated, conserved and scientifically analyzed a few years ago.[16] This spectacular find, in which the deceased had been found lying on an extraordinary bronze 'sofa', wearing some kind of 'Vietnamese-style' hat, made of birch bark, himself covered with gold, displayed all the features that I had been observing in my own series of funerary assemblages. Depending on their nature and their position within the funerary chamber, the various categories of grave goods were associated with different durations. Of course, all of these things had been put in at one single moment in time, when the grave had been constituted, but some pieces were already nearly a century old when they were placed into the chamber; while some others probably dated back to a few decades before and yet others had just been made specially for the burial. In other words, most of the grave goods hadn't belong to the deceased: the funerary assemblage was a *collage* of pieces from different times, different origins, with different meanings.

But more interestingly, all of this was *stratified*. The grave good assemblage had been constructed in the course of at least three different episodes, which were recognizable on the artefacts themselves: during episode 2a, for instance, the dagger, the belt plaque and the shoes of the dead had been covered with ornamented gold leaf. But stratification was also indirect, although also printed into matter. The funerary chamber, for instance, was divided into two different parts: one for the body and the other for the accompanying grave goods, such as a four-wheeled wagon containing the horse harness and a set of bronze vessels. This was a distinctive local feature, usually associated with cremation graves in the 8th to 7th century BC. This old-fashioned style funerary chamber had received an inhumation, which was combined with the specific modes of deposition of personal grave goods characterizing this funerary feature, introduced in this region at the beginning of the 6th century BC. And finally, the chamber had been furnished, aiming to reproduce the arrangement of a rich room – translating locally a Mediterranean fashion from the very end of the 6th century BC.

All of that was encapsulated, as some sort of internal 'material memory', at the moment when the Hochdorf funerary chamber was built and filled, around 500 BC. But how to represent, in our conventional understanding of linear time, these *survivals*? Maybe like this indeed (Figure 1.3):

You recognize here a version of your Husserl's time diagram. But consider this next messy figure now. Do you know where this comes from? (Figure 1.4)

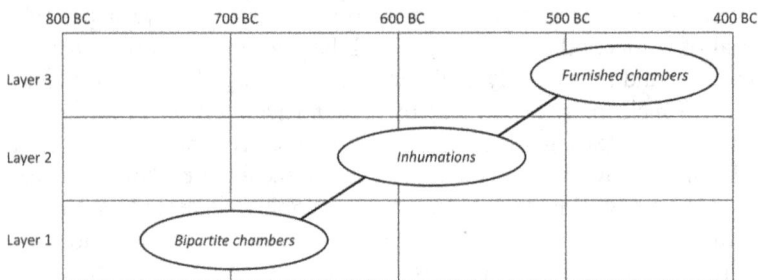

Figure 1.3 A sketch of the stratification of attributes of the funerary chamber in the Hochdorf "princely" grave (after Olivier 1999).

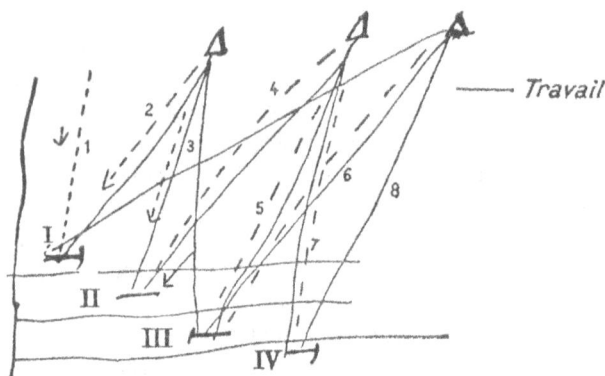

Figure 1.4 Freud's sketch of the structure of the unconscious, 1897 (after Freud, 1956, fig. II).

This is a Sigmund Freud's sketch. He made it on 25 May 1897 in order to explain the structure of the 'hysterical unconscious'.[17] I, II, III and IV are the 'layers' of memory; they have been indeed successively deposited, just as our archaeological layers. But these past depositions are incessantly reinterpreted and reworked afterwards (as denoted by the little triangles). And look, each layer becomes related to the other by this process of re-assessment operating from above.

It works like the Hochdorf funerary chamber. When the grave was put together, its ancient 'layers' were reactivated with a new appearance, like hidden souvenirs; they were put into play again, but in a different context.

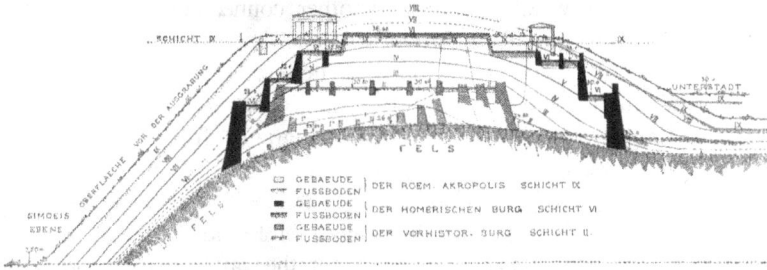

Figure 1.5 Cross-section of the Tell at Troy, as excavated by Heinrich Schliemann (after Dörpfeld, 1902, fig. 6).

They were still here but they meant something slightly different. So, in a way, the past was still acting *across* the accumulation of what had come after, which bore its distinctive imprint. The past *constrains* the future by its *presence*. And it is still present, although transformed and sometimes not recognizable anymore. To put it in another way, the past is pointing towards the future, not primarily as an effect of the course of time but as a product of its reinterpretation. When reinterpretation stops, the past gets frozen. And we can dig it.

You know this other figure (Figure 1.5); this is the section of the Tell of Troy, reproduced in *Troja und Ilion,* published by Wilhelm Dörpfeld in 1902.[18] Freud had this book in his library. This is a sketch, but look at the succession of ramparts, one on top of the other: as in the Hochdorf grave, they are maintaining and 're-interpreting' a feature belonging to a vanished past, whose presence exists only in its remembrance: an ancient fortified city, deeply buried in the ground.

And all of this succession happens in the 'present': the different presents that have come afterwards, during which these old remains have been reactivated, and our present, now, in which the site of Troy is still standing. It is Freud who helped me to understand that the key question of archaeology was not the past *per se,* but the *memory of the past* – since the past had been incessantly reworked by the process of memory itself. And again it was Freud who convinced me that the location of the past in this different approach wasn't some imaginary place in the past – as we are used to considering it in archaeology: the Neolithic, the Iron Age, the Middle age ... – but the present itself, or more precisely what may be called the 'après-coup' of the past.

Gavin: Freud's sketch is incredible and makes me wonder the extent to which Husserl and Freud may have been aware of each others work or whether there is another connecting link. Husserl's diagrams date from 1905-7 so somewhat later than the Freud diagram you showed, but both thinkers drew on the work of Brentano and possibly there is a common source here as Brentano was using similar diagrams from 1873.[19] But whatever the story behind these diagrams, the way we came to similar conclusions from two different directions is very interesting. Of course the interest of Freud in archaeology is well known and as you pointed out, the way the past carries over into the present in archaeology does share many affinities with Freud's notion of memory and the unconscious. Although I was also reading some Freud at the time, I did not make any of the connections you did. My closest brush to your concerns was in a paper I published just after my PhD called 'Forgetting the Past' where I basically said archaeology was *nothing* like memory as Freud discussed; that the deep past, prehistory comprised a radical forgetting, that it is a past that was never ours to remember.[20] I am not sure how I feel about this paper today – there are some nice poetic moments in it, but my main argument was more about prehistory as an alien past and how we confront that fact. This was in part, the influence of Ricoeur, Heidegger and Levinas and the connection between alterity and time. What escaped me completely here was the deeper mechanisms of time and memory that Freud was using and which you picked up on.

Notes

1. L. Olivier, *The Shapes of Time. An Archaeology of the Early Iron Age Funerary Assemblages in the West Hallstatt Province* (Unpublished PhD Dissertation, University of Cambridge, 1994).
2. G. Lucas, 'The Changing Face of Time: English Domestic Clocks from the Seventeenth to Nineteenth Century', *Journal of Design History* 8 (1995): 1–9.
3. G. Kubler, *The Shape of Time. Remarks on the History of Things* (New Haven: Yale University Press, 1962).
4. E. Dethlefsen and J. Deetz, 'Death's Heads, Cherubs, and Willow Trees: Experimental Archaeology in Colonial Cemeteries'. *American Antiquity*, 31, no.4 (1966): 502–510.
5. G. Lucas, Genealogies. Classification, Narrative and Time: An Archaeological Study of Eastern Yorkshire, 3700-1300 BC (Unpublished PhD Dissertation, University of Cambridge, 1994).
6. A. Leroi-Gourhan, *Les fouilles préhistoriques. Technique et méthodes* (Paris: A et J. Picard, 1950).
7. M. Julien, C. Karlin, P. Bodu, « Pincevent: où en est le modèle théorique aujourd'hui? », *Bulletin de la Société préhistorique française*, 1987, vol. 84, n° 10–12, *Hommage de la SPF à André Leroi-Gourhan*, pp. 335–342.

8. A. Leroi-Gourhan and M. Brézillon, *Fouilles de Pincevent. Essai d'analyse ethnographique d'un habitat magdalénien* (Paris, éditions du CNRS, VIIème supplément à Gallia Préhistoire, 1972). Also see F. Audouze, 'Leroi-Gourhan, a Philosopher of Technique and Evolution'. *Journal of Archaeological Research* 10, no. 4, (2002): 277–306.

9. J. McGlade, The emergence of structure: modelling social transformation in later Prehistoric Wessex (Unpublished PhD dissertation. Cambridge, University of Cambridge, 1990).

10. E. Husserl, *The Phenomenology of Internal Time-Consciousness* (Bloomington: Indiana University Press, 1966).

11. See A. Schnapp., *La conquête du passé. Aux origines de l'archéologie* (Paris: Dominique Carré, 2020).

12. A. Schnapp (ed.), *L'archéologie aujourd'hui* (Paris, Hachette, 1980).

13. M. Schiffer, *Behavioural Archaeology* (New York, Academic Press, 1976); L. Binford, "Behavioral Archaeology and the Pompeii Premise," *Journal of Anthropological Research* 37 (1981): 195–208; Schiffer Michael B., *Formation Processes of the Archaeological Record* (Albuquerque, University of New Mexico, 1987).

14. F. Bordes, "Sur la notion de sol d'habitat en préhistoire paléolithique", *Bulletin de la Société préhistorique française* 72, no.5 (1975): 139–144.

15. Where the department of Archaeology at Cambridge was located.

16. L. Olivier, "The Tomb of Hochdorf (Baden-Wurttemberg): some comments on the nature of archaeological funerary material," *Archaeological Review from Cambridge* 11, no. 1 (1992): 51–63. I have presented a more detailed study of this case in: "The Hochdorf princely grave and the question of the nature of archaeological funerary assemblages," in *Time and Archaeology*, ed. Murray T (London and New York, Routledge, 1999), 109–138.

17. S. Freud, *La naissance de la psychanalyse* (French translation by Marie Bonaparte, Anna Freud and Ernst Kris. Paris: Presses universitaires de France, 1956).

18. W. Dörpfeld, *Troja und Ilion. Ergebnisse der Ausgrabungen in der vorhistorischen und historischen Schichten von Ilion, 1870-1894* (Athens, Beck & Barth 1902).

19. F. Brentano, *Philosophical Investigations on Space, Time and Continuum* (London: Routledge, 2010); also see J. Dodd, .Reading Husserl's Time-Diagrams from 1917/18, *Husserl Studies* 21 (2005): 111–137.

20. G. Lucas, 1997. Forgetting the Past, *Anthropology Today*, 13: 8–14.

Bibliography

Audouze, F., 'Leroi-Gourhan, a Philosopher of Technique and Evolution'. *Journal of Archaeological Research* 10 no. 4, (2002): 277–306.

Binford L. 'Behavioral Archaeology and the Pompeii Premise', *Journal of Anthropological Research* 37 (1981): 195–208.

Bordes, F. 'Sur la notion de sol d'habitat en préhistoire paléolithique', *Bulletin de la Société préhistorique française* 72, no.5, (1975): 139–144.

Brentano F. *Philosophical Investigations on Space, Time and Continuum.* London: Routledge, 2010.

Dethlefsen, E., and Deetz, J. 'Death's Heads, Cherubs, and Willow Trees: Experimental Archaeology in Colonial Cemeteries'. *American Antiquity* 31, no. 4, (1966): 502–510.

Dörpfeld W. *Troja und Ilion. Ergebnisse der Ausgrabungen in der vorhistorischen und historischen Schichten von Ilion, 1870–1894*. Athens: Beck & Barth, 1902.

Dodd, J. Reading Husserl's Time-Diagrams from 1917/18. *Husserl Studies*, 21 (2005): 111–137.

Freud S. *La naissance de la psychoanalyse*. French translation by Marie Bonaparte, Anna Freud and Ernst Kris. Paris: Presses universitaires de France, 1956.

Husserl, E. *The Phenomenology of Internal Time-Consciousness*. Bloomington: Indiana University Press, 1966.

Julien, M., Karlin, C., Bodu, P., Pincevent: où en est le modèle théorique aujourd'hui?, *Bulletin de la Société préhistorique française* 84, no. 10–12, (1987), *Hommage de la SPF à André Leroi-Gourhan*, 335–42.

Kubler, G. *The Shape of Time. Remarks on the History of Things*. New Haven: Yale University Press, 1962.

Leroi-Gourhan, A. *Les fouilles préhistoriques. Technique et méthodes*. Paris: A et J. Picard, 1950.

Leroi-Gourhan, A. and Brézillon, M. *Fouilles de Pincevent. Essai d'analyse ethnographique d'un habitat magdalénien*. Paris, éditions du CNRS, VIIème supplément à Gallia Préhistoire, 1972.

Lucas, G. Genealogies Classification, Narrative and Time: An Archaeological Study of Eastern Yorkshire, 3700-1300 BC. Unpublished PhD Dissertation, University of Cambridge, 1994.

Lucas, G. 'The Changing Face of Time: English Domestic Clocks from the Seventeenth to Nineteenth Century', *Journal of Design History*, 8 (1995): 1–9.

Lucas, G. Forgetting the Past. *Anthropology Today*, 13 (1997): 8–14.

McGlade J. The emergence of structure: modelling social transformation in later Prehistoric Wessex. Unpublished PhD dissertation. Cambridge: University of Cambridge, 1990.

Olivier, L. 'The Tomb of Hochdorf (Baden-Wurttemberg): some comments on the nature of archaeological funerary material', *Archaeological Review from Cambridge* 11, no. 1, (1992): 51–63.

Olivier, L. *The Shapes of Time. An Archaeology of the Early Iron Age Funerary Assemblages in the West Hallstatt Province*. Unpublished PhD Dissertation, University of Cambridge, 1994.

Olivier, L. 'The Hochdorf princely grave and the question of the nature of archaeological funerary assemblages', in Murray T. (ed.), *Time and Archaeology*. London and New York: Routledge, 1999, pp. 109–138.

Schiffer M.B. *Behavioral Archaeology*. New York, Academic Press, 1976.

Schiffer M.B. *Formation Processes of the Archaeological Record*. Albuquerque: University of New Mexico, 1987.

Schnapp A. (ed.), *L'archéologie aujourd'hui*. Paris: Hachette, 1980.

Schnapp, A., *La conquête du passé. Aux origines de l'archéologie*. Paris: Dominique Carré, 2020.

2 Life after Cambridge

Archaeology is often described as a discipline that deals with the past, yet as other archaeologists have noted, we don't have access to the past – only what remains of the past in the present. But recognition of this has much more serious implications that we often give credit for. The present is, paradoxically, the only place the past – in whatever shape or form – actually exists as Laurent touched on in the last chapter. This property of 'remaining' is critical to archaeology, not just as a methodological issue, but as a substantial matter of writing and interpretation. How does what survive or remain, affect the shape of our archaeological accounts of the past? This is not just about how we interpret the past from what survives, but more importantly, how the historical process itself is shaped by the materiality of 'remaining'. In the years after his PhD, Laurent explored these issues both through the writings of Walter Benjamin who suggests a very different way to write about the past to conventional history, and through the work of the French school of archaeogeography. After a hiatus, Gavin too began to engage with the same issues, but through a critical engagement with the work of time perspectivism and exploring the temporal structure of the archaeological record.

Gavin: In many ways, after I finished my PhD I put time aside for the next decade or so. I wrote a short textbook on time in archaeology which came out in 2005, but this drew heavily on the background reading I had done for my PhD and apart from a little additional material on time perspectivism and palimpsests, there was nothing especially novel in it – for me at least.[1] I did not intellectually return to time until after this book came out, so 12 or 13 years after my PhD. Instead, I became more interested in the nature of archaeological fieldwork and the archaeological process, probably because after my PhD, after a few half-hearted and failed attempts to get an academic post, I returned to commercial archaeology. I remember one particularly dismal moment when I got a part time job in adult education at London's Birkbeck College outreach department. I slaved away preparing my lectures and turned up on my first evening to find one student had enrolled. They had to cancel the course and the truth is, I was deeply relieved. I pretty much decided an academic post was not for me and after some short-term work for archaeological units in London, I returned to Cambridge to work for Chris Evans and the departmental archaeology unit.

DOI: 10.4324/9781003183600-2

And I loved it. It was both socially and intellectually a great environment and I found I could still write papers and even a book while doing commercial archaeology. But this was a special place and very unlike most commercial units in England at that time – and possibly still today.

Laurent: The return to real life was difficult for me as well. I got my job back at the Ministry of Culture and a position at the regional archaeological service in Orléans. It was both boring, time-consuming and stressing. My work was to examine the applications for construction permits, to check if there was any archaeological remains around, or the likelihood thereof, and, in such cases, to order test-trenching. Then, if the trenching would have revealed any archaeological activity, I had to recommend the opening of an excavation (or not), writing a report to a (then) commission that would decide if this operation should be carried out (or not). It was all about procedures and no one was interested in knowing what I had learnt about archaeological time or even how it was to study in such an exotic place as Cambridge.

They were difficult times at home too. I had been back from Cambridge since the summer, when in the fall my mother was diagnosed with cancer. Six months later she was dead, being only 62, when my wife Anne was pregnant with our first child, Rémi. I became an orphan at the age of 37, having already lost my father twelve years before. Cancer again. So I had to do what everyone has to do at some point in his or her life: empty the house of my dead parents, throw away what I could not keep, sell what I could, and keep for myself the few things that I was able to retain. Which is to say, almost nothing. Doing this is just like destroying yourself, your own past. It deeply affected me, more than I realized at that time.

But finally I was lucky enough to find a position at the National Museum of Archaeology in Saint-Germain-en-Laye, where I am still working today. The position of the curator for Celtic and Gallic Archaeology had become available there, as my predecessor had left for another place. I applied and I got the job. It changed my life. This museum was created in 1862 by the emperor Napoleon III and holds truly extraordinary collections; it is also an amazing place to study the history of the archaeological discipline in France and abroad, since it houses huge archives. I was finally relieved from this administrative burden to which the practice of archaeology had been reduced in the archaeological services.

And what about you; how did you reconnect with time? Could you explain which new elements you put into your 2005 book, compared to the ideas you had developed in your PhD? And how did you move forward from that point?

Gavin: It was a long process. I was in commercial archaeology for around six happy years, but inevitably perhaps, the edge gradually came off the excitement and pleasure of my job. It wasn't that I got tired of fieldwork or my colleagues, it was more that I was starting to feel the need for more time and space to do research and writing. As I mentioned, the Cambridge Unit was an exceptional place in giving one that freedom, but necessarily there were limits; at the end of the day, finishing a job, writing the report came first. It meant I still had to spend evenings and weekends working on my own projects. At first, I took unpaid leave to quench this thirst; I got funding to run a three-year project in South Africa so for three summers I went there to excavate post 17th century sites. (I should say here also that even before I had handed in my PhD, my interests were turning away from prehistory and into historical archaeology). I also went to join my former supervisor Ian Hodder on the Çatalhöyük project for two summers and then to Iceland to run a field school for an old friend from my undergraduate days. But all this did was accumulate more work outside my 'day job'. Then, a larger opportunity suddenly opened up in Iceland: come and run a large excavation in the summer and so long as the post-excavation work was maintained, I could spend the rest of the year doing my own research. This was like a golden ticket and even though it meant a major move, I don't think there was any question of turning it down. I was single, having just split up from my girlfriend and had no ties to keep me in England.

So I ended up in Iceland in 2002 and there, I suddenly had time to write. I wrote two books in a fairly short span; one was based on my work in South Africa,[2] the other though was this book on time.[3] So now I finally get to answering your question. I must admit I had to flick through this book to remind myself what I had written and in places, I was quite surprised. As I mentioned, a lot was drawn on background reading and thinking for my PhD, but this was not an edited version of my PhD by any sense. I was commissioned to write a general textbook, introducing students and scholars to the issues and debates around the topic. So what I did was structure it around a very simple idea: that the problem of time was not as straightforward as simply trying to improve our dating techniques. Each chapter tried to explore a different facet of time, but the two central chapters revolved around time in the archaeological record and time as it was perceived or experienced in past societies. In a way, both of these were new elements as neither formed a core part of my PhD research, although elements of both were incorporated into it. Of these two themes though, it was the former that was to take on greater importance and in fact my interest in time perception in the past quickly receded.

So what was novel in my interest in time and the archaeological record? As I mentioned previously, it was the ideas of time perspectivism, the notion of palimpsests and especially your own work, which for the first time I properly engaged with, particularly the study on the Hochdorf grave which appeared in an edited volume by Tim Murray from 1999. Perversely, I was never aware of its earlier incarnation in the *Archaeological Review from Cambridge*, underlining how compartmentalized I was. In fact, it was in part because of increasing contacts and meetings with Tim Murray that I was taken in this direction. It was only while I was doing commercial archaeology for the Cambridge Archaeology Unit that I got to know Tim through Chris Evans (director of the Unit), and ironically, largely because of our common interest in historical archaeology not time.

The key thing though was how all this work seemed to readily connect with my earlier studies on design and form, and how the same issues which beset my study of artefact typologies – the articulation of continuity and change and the persistence of the past into later presents – were also at work on sites and in landscapes. I had already started to make such connections through my work on fieldwork and stratigraphy,[4] especially in my first book, but now the same issues were spreading and recurring in all kinds of new contexts. Indeed, looking in that book, I am even struck by a discussion I make on Roman pottery which exactly mirrors what you were saying about the miner's lamps; how our typological dating was off and needed calibrating to make it align with conventional dates (Figure 2.1). How one forgets!

But all this was a very gradual snowball. These themes did not dominate the 2005 book on time; the conclusion to that book rather re-iterated all the points I made in the paper on memory and alterity from 1997. Which is why I suppose I still think of this book as somewhat dated, even when it came out!

But you also had a book on time that came out soon after, although it was not translated into English until even later. Can you tell me about the

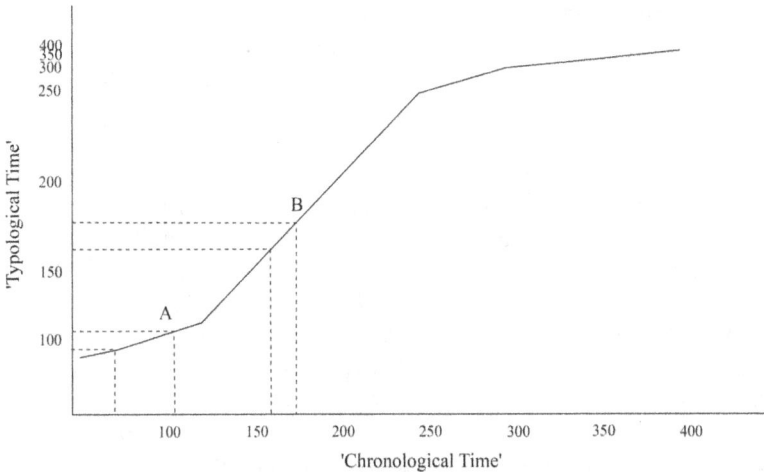

Figure 2.1 The difference between chronological and typological time (after Lucas 2005, fig. 4.4).

genesis of your book and how it connected or departed from your PhD research?

Laurent: Like you, it took me about ten years to begin to put things together with the question of time in archaeology, as this wasn't the primary topic of my PhD which was rather Iron Age funerary assemblages. Whether at the Regional Archaeological Service or at the Saint-Germain museum, I was absorbed then by other tasks: ordering the collections, organizing exhibitions, setting research studies on our series ... and diving into the fabulous 19th century archives of the *Musée des Antiquités nationales*, later renamed in *Musée d'Archéologie nationale*.[5]

Meanwhile the little group of 'The Parisians' had a plan for Sander: to have him come to Paris and teach at the Paris-Sorbonne University and reframe the teaching of archaeology around him. The idea was also to recruit some of his PhD students to contribute to this new syllabus – for instance with archaeological epistemology, which would have been my subject. To put it frankly, it was a coup. And it completely failed, making Sander and Anick leave for the States.

But at that moment, I still had to get a final qualification in order to be able to supervise PhD students as a professor: what is called in the

French academic system *Habilitation à Diriger des Recherches* (HDR). This is a short piece of work, of about 50,000 words, in which you summarize your research history: where you come from, what you have been doing and which perspectives you are presently planning to develop for the future. So I wrote it in 2004.[6] And it was a shorter version of this dissertation that was later published in 2008 at the Seuil editing house, in the same series where Paul Ricoeur, Cornelius Castoradis or Slavoj Žižek had earlier published their work.[7]

So what do you get inside this book? Basically a study of the relationship between archaeological remains and time, based on a synthesis of the results that I obtained from my PhD as well as a couple of new ideas. We have already talked about our Cambridge years, but what emerged from this time is this issue we were both gravitating around, like two different little asteroids: that archaeological time and chronological time are two different dimensions, one is real and the other abstract. The real one is not the one we would usually think of: it is archaeological time, as a product of materiality.

This is the real physical time; the other being just a convention, a mode of measurement, a scale in other words. So this is the reason why it is fundamentally important to focus our attention onto archaeological remains and look at their behavior in archaeological time: how their accumulation constructs in fact a material memory of the past, which is the true subject of archaeology. This point was already present in some form in my earlier doctoral dissertation *Shapes of Time*, written at Cambridge.

But re-reading this HDR work more than 15 years later, I also see a new concept emerging there: the present as being the location of the past. I know that this sounds foolish, since our immediate perception of time is chronological – for us, the past is necessarily *before* the present; it has happened while the present *is happening*. As stressed by Bergson though, this perception is just one of the two dimensions of time; the other being that of *duration* – that is to say our archaeological time.[8] If you take seriously enough this observation that real time is the material time of archaeological remains, the present – I mean our present, just now, here – isn't anymore what is happening at the moment: it is what is *remaining* at the moment, around us, in the ground under our feet, and above us, in the starry sky. It is all the durations of the past – from the birth of the universe to your immediate material environment: the chair on which you are seated, your clothes, and even yourself, as a body. All of that is physically co-present, and this is the very reason why we can dig into the past: it is still there, as a material presence. It has ceased to be but it hasn't ceased to exist.

The other new idea, compared to my earlier *Shapes of Time*, was epistemology; in a way this is maybe not so far from your own interest in the perception of time by past societies. It is based on this very simple idea: if the past is what materially remains within the present, so it has always been a phenomenon that people have been experiencing, from prehistory to modern times. In this respect, the history of archaeology is basically the history of this confrontation with material time. How indeed did people perceive and explain it? What did they notice, or what did they ignore? It took me a long time, but it is at that point that I began to carefully read philosophy: I finally had got a point of view from which to look at it.

And you? How did you move from your earlier work?

Gavin: It was really by getting deep into the nature of the archaeological record. I started to re-visit very old discussions in formation theory, especially from within processual archaeology about how complex and multi-layered even a single archaeological feature could be. In a way, I was starting to explore the same problems you had with your Hochdorf grave ten or fifteen years earlier. I was interested in the different temporalities of deposits and assemblages, and within assemblages, issues of use life, discard rates and so on. Like you and your disillusionment with '*le patron*' Leroi-Gourhan's goal of creating an ethnographic archaeology, I was deeply troubled by this, although the instigation for me came from Tim Murray and the arguments of time perspectivism as developed by Geoff Bailey.[9] They too suggested that an ethnographic archaeology was impossible given the nature of the archaeological record which they saw as too coarse-grained, temporally speaking, to offer the kind of resolution needed to do ethnographic-style archaeology. Rather it offered better potential for drawing out longer-term processes and structures. So you see it took me a decade or more to catch up with where you were in the 1990s.

At the same time, I was not quite convinced of the arguments of time perspectivism. As far as I was concerned, there were lots of good examples showing how archaeology could do an ethnography. More to the point, I felt this critique of an 'ethnographic archaeology' or 'palaeo-ethnography', rather misrepresented ethnography. This assumption that somehow ethnography dealt in lived time, that it offered snapshots – these assumptions which lay behind the arguments of time perspectivism, didn't ring true to me. Yes, ethnographers worked in real time with subjects who lived in real time, but their ethnographies were commonly abstractions, attempts to understand the deeper cultural logic of a society, whether this was through the structuralism of Lévi-Strauss or the functionalism of Malinowski and Radcliffe-Brown. What they produced were route maps for understanding a culture which transcended the time in which they were constructed. Yes, this also resulted in that fiction of the 'ethnographic present' – a time which is stretched without specific duration, a time where nothing changes and after Fabian, might be cast as another or parallel time to the ethnographer. But that is another issue; the point here is archaeologists were doing the same with past societies. We weren't trying to reconstruct snapshots, to re-create a lived time of ethnography at all. We were just trying to understand the cultural logic of past communities, and like ethnographers, our work also occurred in real time.

So for me, the issue was not how to develop an archaeology where time was fundamentally different from 'real time' or ethnographic time. I wanted to understand rather how archaeological time was possible at all – because if one took the arguments of time perspectivism to the extreme, it suggested the archaeological record should not really make any sense at all. It should just be random noise. Yet we do discern pattern and order; how is that possible? Initially at least, for me the answer to this question lay in understanding how things *resisted* entropy – how they managed to persist in the archaeological record and why some things persisted and others didn't. Yes, the past does carry over into the present, but *selectively* so. This was more than a matter of physical decay, of perishability. For me it was about irreversibility; about the irreversibility and inertia built into material systems. A common example I used was the traffic system and how difficult it is to change the UK system of driving on the left to the right, in conformity with the rest of Europe. This is not simply a matter of habit – or human behavioral habit. It was equally if not more about material 'habit' and what was needed to make such a change – steering wheels on cars, traffic signs, road systems. To make such a change requires great physical effort in undoing what already exists.

Comparing my trajectory to yours, it seems we truly moved in parallel yet inverted ways; we were both working towards the same issues but whereas you began from archaeology and moved towards philosophy, it seems I did it the other way around. So perhaps you can tell me more of the philosophy you were reading now and how specifically it helped.

Laurent: Oh yes indeed, we did! When you were deconstructing the notion of archaeological record, I was, at that moment, looking for echoes of what I had seen about archaeological time in the works of people who had been already encountering this strange behavior of materiality. I had already read them separately, but for the first time I was able to see how complementary these people were; their works forming some sort of abstract constellation.

The brightest star, for me, was obviously Walter Benjamin and his *Theses on the Philosophy of History*. In his powerful and poetic language, he put words on the weird trajectories of the archaeological record I had been observing. Focusing his attention on the materiality of history – exploring the many covered streets or arcades (the *passages*), in his contemporary Paris of the 1920s, as a fossilized product of the 19th century – Benjamin rejected the conventional approach of history, in which each new event wipes out the previous one.[10] Above all, he presented this rejection of historicism as a political fight against conservatism and Fascism. According to Benjamin, the past isn't only defined by its encapsulation in the past – as was the claim of the historicists – but it emerges within the present, as a kind of active memory. I cannot resist quoting his 18th thesis, which can be read as a manifesto for an anti-historicist archaeology: Historicism contents itself with establishing a causal connection between various moments in history. But no fact that is a cause is for that very reason historical. It became historical posthumously, as it were, through events that may be separated from it by thousands of years. A historian who takes this as his point of departure stops telling the sequence of events like the beads of a rosary. Instead, he grasps the constellation which his own era has formed with a definite earlier one. Thus he establishes a conception of the present as the 'time of the now' which is shot through with chips of Messianic time.

Close to Benjamin followed Aby Warburg, another bizarre German thinker. An Art historian, he theorized in the 1920s on survival effects (*Nachleben*) in artistic representations, elaborating a typology of 'forms of pathos' (*Pathosformen*) expressed across time, from antiquity to modern times, in sculpture and painting. This was a mad project of course, gathering all the images produced across the world and connecting them, looking for the reappearance of ancient forms under a new aspect: the *Mnenosyne Atlas*.[11]

Why do things keep coming back? It is a 'biological necessity', wrote Warburg, 'between instinct and destructive logic'. There is a secret link between the insane Warburg – he suffered schizophrenia –

and Henri Focillon, the French Art historian we mentioned earlier. Studying Medieval sculpture, Focillon noticed that a similar pattern of sequences tends to appear over time in stylistic creations, no matter what their position within chronological time: a first phase of experiencing the creation of new forms, a second one, during which forms are stabilized, and a final episode, in the course of which forms tends to hypertrophy: that is to say the typical sequence of *archaic*, *classic* and *baroque*. This is not just a stylistic chronology, according to Focillon: this is a search – a search for the new *in* the old, exploring the potentialities offered by artistic materiality.[12] Stylistic time is basically unstable, independent of chronological time – just like archaeological time.

But tell me more about what you worked on after Cambridge …

Gavin: It was really my interest in the archaeological record that got me back into time, especially through re-engaging with formation theory and time perspectivism, as I mentioned earlier. I circled repeatedly around these issues of irreversibility and entropy in various publications[13] in the years after my 2005 book on time and felt there was a deeper lesson here about archaeology and history, but it always seemed to elude my grasp. In a way, what I wanted to say was that the things that have survived or persisted into the present, in the archaeological record or even in our everyday world, have done so not through chance but because they are deeply significant. Persistence is not simply a physical property but an historical one. This was a gloss on Childe's view about understanding past societies – instead of Hawkes ladder of inference[14] where ideas were the hardest part of past societies to access, Childe argued that rather it is only the *failed* ideas that we cannot understand; the successes have been passed on and are still alive with us today, and it is that aspect of past mentalities that we can still grasp because we share them with our prehistoric ancestors.[15] This view – which was informed both by an evolutionary view of ideology being subject to natural selection, but also of a Marxist view of true and false consciousness (science vs. ideology) – is of course deeply problematic but in rejecting its evolutionary and Marxist overtones as I did, one also loses any reason for believing it. I guess my ultimate motive here was to demonstrate that we should not bemoan the fragmentary nature of the archaeological record. That its very fragmentary nature, its partial preservation, is due to a kind of 'natural' selection process, but rather than being about a selection informed by adaptation or fitness or 'truth', it was one informed by a social or historical resistance to entropy. If this makes sense!

Anyhow, I gave up this chimera as at the end of day, it still felt rather arbitrary and frankly untrue. Instead, I moved to another issue, that of contemporaneity. In part, this also addressed the issue of the persistence of the past into the present, but instead of looking at it historically as I had in terms of entropy and irreversibility, I looked at it in terms of the juxtaposition of past and present and the different ways this juxtaposition might be articulated. I published a paper on this in 2015 in *Archaeological Dialogues* and you were one of the commentators of course.[16] There, I tried to reflect on how we might think about contemporaneity as a different way to write about the past; not really as the past in our present (archaeology reduced to heritage really), but as about any present – whether this was the 'present' of 4000 BC or 1650 AD. You see despite everything, I did and still do cling to the old ambition of archaeology which is to 'reconstruct' or 'resurrect' the past – although this way of phrasing is, I know, problematic. Maybe a better word is re-presencing the past. This isn't about trying to go back in time, as in a time machine to 1650 AD; it's rather about trying to create an imaginary (but not fictive as in untrue) 'present', where 1650 lives as a fragile bubble within 2020. After all, isn't this what happens when we handle a pot from the 17th century today? All I wanted to do was to see archaeology like this, and for me, writing can do this and do it best.

But now I fear I am getting ahead of myself as I am not sure I would have articulated it quite like this back in 2015. It is only since revisiting the topic of writing and especially the links between time and narrative that were a core part of my PhD, that I see things this way.[17] It was a slow process. But at the same time, it is quite pleasing that I find myself returning to issues like narrative and time that were a major focus of my doctoral research 25 years ago and have now come back again. It was also around this time of course that our paths finally crossed again. You first invited me to your workshop in Metz on archaeologies of the contemporary past in 2014 and then in 2017 I invited you to Reykjavík for a Nordic graduate seminar workshop on time. These two occasions were enough to rekindle an old association and for me at least, your recent work on time continues to provoke and stimulate me, not least your engagement with Hartog's presentism which I first encountered at the Metz workshop.

But how would you sum up how your thoughts have developed since Cambridge and especially your 2008 book?

Laurent: My '*Dark abyss of Time*' was an attempt to answer to Benjamin's call to give up with historicism in archaeology; it was a rebellion against the conventional approach of the archaeological discipline, which aims to reach the past 'as it really was'. I was full of anger and dissatisfaction when writing this book, realizing that archaeology was basically founded on such an anti-revolutionary approach of time. So I just did my best to demolish it, down to the ground. And some people said: - Well, you've broken it, but what are you going to build in its place? They were right, and by the way this is precisely what you pointed out in your comment of the book when it was first published.[18]

But you know, things happen in their own way, sometimes beyond our awareness. A few years earlier, I had been very lucky to be asked to set up a field research project in Eastern France, on a series of Iron Age saltworks known as the '*Briquetage de la Seille*'.[19] I was provided with a pretty good amount of money, coming both from the State and the Moselle department, renewable every year. It has lasted over more than 15 years, only ending in 2017 when my research project reached its end – quite an unimaginable situation today.

These sites were rather difficult to dig, since they were huge and also deeply buried under alluvial deposits, in a marshy environment that had been drained only at the beginning of the 20th century. So we began with geophysics, coring and geo-archaeology, in order to get first a global picture both in space and time, focusing our attention on the relationship between archaeological sites and the transformations of the local natural environment. I was just at the beginning of this project when I wrote my *Dark abyss of Time*.

What we soon discovered was completely unexpected: these salt-works extended sometimes over several kilometers in length, having ejected into this small valley millions of cubic meters of industrial refuse; but they had also dramatically transformed their natural en-vironment in the course of a few centuries.[20] Throwing their waste of debris of salt moulds and furnaces directly into the channels of the little Seille river and deforesting the hills around to produce charcoal for their kilns, these people had produced a combination of severe floods and strong erosion, gradually filling the valley, which was rapidly transformed into a huge marsh.

The Iron Age people responded to this by increasing the accumulation of industrial waste above the level of the floodplain, creating artificial mounds several meters high. But the situation became clearly catastrophic in the course of the 5th century BC: they had to abandon most of their production sites scattered in the valley, and concentrate their production onto a few major mounds, some of those reaching still today up to 12 meters high and around 500 meters in diameter. They were the only ones to resist this irresistible degradation of the local environment and so they were transformed into urban agglomerations during the Roman period, then medieval cities and today modern hamlets.

I apologize for this long introduction, but this research pushed me to approach these Iron Age saltworks in a different way to the usual sites of this period. They had experienced what may be called a critical 'post-history', which had imposed a series of *constraints* on subsequent archaeological settlements: in other words, the structure of the Roman or medieval cities built on these major Iron Age mounds had to be understood as an *effect* of the Iron Age impact on the landscape. In the same way, the immense marsh that you can see on the maps of those places in the 17th and 18th centuries has to be seen as a resilient product of the disturbance of the river environment created more than two millennia earlier.

There are even some more puzzling facts, when you are aware of this very long history of the valley, that we have been able to reconstruct since the beginning of the Holocene, around 10,000 BC. In the 1780s, the social and economic situation of France was so bad that everywhere, in every village and every city, people gathered their complaints in notebooks, called *cahiers de doléances*, which were sent to the king. Everywhere, people complained about taxes and the privileges of the lords, except in this part of the Seille valley. There, people complained about the marsh, which was maintained by the Army as a natural defence to protect the fortified places where salt is still produced, on the very same places as the Late Iron Age.

The inhabitants said that the maintenance of the marsh affected the poorest people of their communities, throwing them into misery: their cows had no grass to eat, people were getting sick with 'marsh fever' and died quickly, every year; there was no wood to heat their houses – since it was requisitioned for the salterns – and babies had died from coldness in their beds... All of that because of the marsh; so they urged the authorities to drain the valley, for the benefit of everyone. From an archaeological point of view, this is fascinating: an artificial disturbance of the natural environment created from the 6th century BC is contributing to a social and economic disorder at the end of the 18th century AD, feeding a pre-revolutionary situation, which is enhanced by two previous years of a climatic depression producing bad harvests.

So I became interested in the 'masked effects' of the past, as a lasting presence. It is a major feature in landscapes studies, as the French school of 'archaeo-geography' has demonstrated, especially through Gérard Chouquer's works.[21] They have coined a strange word to describe this phenomenon: *transformission*, which is a combination of *transmission* and *transformation* – meaning that the features of the past are transmitted while being transformed. Very interestingly, *transformission* is also a recurrent pattern observed by psychoanalysis, which deals with memory and the unconscious. So does it mean that common mechanisms operate both in the construction of the psychic memory of the unconscious and in the material memory of the landscape – that is to say in archaeological matter?[22]

But there is another important lesson that the *Briquetage de la Seille* project taught me. As archaeologists, we are not outside of this process: we are directly engaged with it. Indeed, we were able to survey and excavate those sites that had been abandoned in the 5th century BC – since they were never re-occupied afterwards. But this wasn't the case with the major mounds of the late Iron Age, which were covered by several meters of urban stratigraphic layers and located under the present villages, where it was just impossible to conduct large-scale excavation. So, our research project itself was also modelled by constraints inherited from the remote past of the Iron Age. We were part of this construction over time, which was also providing the conditions for the creation of a narrative of this history.

So you see, following different lines, I came across similar issues: the 'resilient past'; irreversibility and the question of archaeological contemporaneity, the interpretation and fiction of the past …

But could you develop these ideas you were exploring in 2010?

Gavin: Your project sounds quite astounding – both in terms of the spatial scale of the impact of these saltworks, but also their temporal reach, the long-term reverberations they have had on local communities ever since, even up to, as you say, the choices facing archaeologists on where to dig. These reverberations you describe are exactly how I have always interpreted Husserl's time diagrams that I mentioned in the last chapter in relation to archaeology; how events from the deep past can still impact and shape people centuries, even millennia later. But you are asking me to expand on my ideas from the around the time of the article on contemporaneity; well I guess the way I saw this was by thinking about past presents as contemporaneous bundles, in the same way you had described our present. From this basis, I asked: how might this change how we write about the past? One of the threads that I really tried to follow was the idea of thinking about the past in terms of a changing configuration of possibilities; what if we wrote about the Iron Age saltworks for example as if we didn't know what happened next? Pick any point in time, any point in the history of this landscape you were excavating – whether 6th century BC, 4th century AD or 18th century – and try to write about it, only with knowledge of what came before, not after. I felt that writing about a site which starts in 6th century BC and ends in the 18th century or the present, has to be different to a story that starts in the 6th century BC and ends in the 5th century AD. How easy is it to 'forget' what comes after? How important is the ending to shaping your narrative? The point of this exercise was in a sense, to try and re-presence a past present without the benefit of hindsight, or rather by putting the question of hindsight up front. Always start with when your story ends, not when it begins. After all, the beginning is usually already decided for you.

I have been playing with this idea for a few years now and have tried to make connections to counterfactual and virtual histories, but not in the sense of 'what if?' history (what if Hitler had died as a teenager or if Germany had won WWII), but rather in the sense of seeing past presents as a space of possibilities, in part framed by their own pasts. The influence here comes more from Deleuze and DeLanda. I have never really taken any of these notions beyond the drawing board; they remain merely ideas. But I suppose in some ways, you could define them as a kind of historicism, in the sense of trying to understand the past in its own terms, not those of the present, which is termed 'presentism' (which of course has a very different meaning to presentism as used by Hartog and yourself). Not that I have this naïve belief that we can re-live the past; again, this isn't about some Collingwoodian re-enactment or historical empathy. It is just about taking into account the positionality of any present vis-à-vis its past and future.

In many ways, my view that archaeology can re-presence the past is also linked to the fieldwork I did when I moved to Iceland. The site I mentioned, when I got the new job and moved to Iceland, was an elite settlement, the residence of a Bishop, a school and ecclesiastical centre called Skálholt. It had been established probably in the 10th century AD, but our excavations only uncovered the last three centuries, from c. 1650–1950. We dug for 6 years and the preservation was incredible; walls standing shoulder high in places, floors intact with enviable organic preservation: wood, leather, clothing even birds eggs which looked as if they had hatched yesterday. This was my Pompeii. Of course I was aware by now of all the problems around making any naïve assumptions; I knew we weren't excavating a snapshot, a moment frozen in time. But I was still working on timescales of decades, alongside a rich documentary archive. This was historical archaeology as good as it gets. On such a site, it is hard not to be focused on the small-scale.

Around the time we finished the excavations though, I also moved to a new job at the University of Iceland. In the end, I could not escape an academic position. I have been at the University of Iceland ever since and consider myself very lucky as it has allowed me to continue to read and write in a context where many of my colleagues at other universities around the world are under ever greater pressure from excessive administration and teaching loads. We are a small department with only about 50 students altogether, undergraduate to doctoral level. But the move into academia came at a good time as it turns out. The financial collapse of 2008 made working in the independent sector far more precarious and also more or less put an end to large-scale archaeological research such as I was doing at Skálholt. Since then, my time spent doing fieldwork has gradually diminished so that today, I do very little and some years none at all. In part, this is due to having three kids - I started to date my future wife while we were both working at Skálholt and my first child was born in the last season of our excavation.

But in relation to fieldwork, I have always thought that our theoretical or philosophical outlook is often influenced by the material we work with; you had vast landscapes and long time-scales, I had a single settlement with a 300-year timespan packed full of rich assemblages. Perhaps it is no surprise we began to look at things differently.

Laurent: 'What if?' is precisely the question that came to my mind towards the end of this *Briquetage de la Seille* research project. Indeed, not as some unwarranted assumption that would make us imagine a completely different history of this region: but what if I hadn't seen what I had observed in the post-history of these places; how would I encompass this Iron Age past? And how about all the data that I haven't seen or been able to find yet; isn't it the case most of the time, since, as archaeologists, we all have this odd habit to cut the past into slices, looking only at the period, the site or the objects we think are interesting? At this point, I began to realize that we basically approach the past through the features of its post-history; that in fact the past makes sense to us not really in itself, but across its later *transformission* – just like memories in our mind.

This gave me the core idea of a book, which I published in 2019 on Vercingétorix, the Gallic chief who fought against the Roman invasion of Gaul by Julius Caesar in 52 BC.[23] Since the 19th century, Vercingétorix has been a national hero, the first personage of French history in fact. But this is not what the book is about: it is an attempt to apply an archaeological approach to the historical sources, seen as a stratification of information and interpretation developed over two millennia about this character and the events surrounding his life.

The conventional approach, from a regular historical point of view, would have been to dig out all these parasitic and subsequent layers, in order to uncover the 'true' historical bedrock, containing the 'authentic' data, or at least the ones closest to the 'historic reality' of this time. But if you do that, you end up with just a handful of sand – a few words about Vercingétorix's family and the fate of his father, who was executed for having tried to reintroduce monarchy among the *Arverni* people. Caesar's text allows you to follow the young Gallic chief for only about 9 months, from the winter of 53-52 BC to the fall of 52 BC … and that's it. And of course, all these events are seen from a Roman point of view and by a man, Caesar, who is trying to justify his personal behavior, which was totally illegal in terms of Roman law: even as a governor of a province, you were not allowed to declare war on your own and to use the army of the State to fight allies of the Roman people. So what to do, in this situation? Just what historians have been repeatedly doing: you have to reconstruct a complete world around these tiny scattered bits of data, developing very risky and fragile global assumptions: in a word, you have to create a whole fictitious past.

On the other hand, if you look at what came afterwards in the historical record, you find a very rich and diverse body of data. Since the

Roman period, every generation of historians has been re-inventing its own past, adding details or changing the meaning of the original events. So, just like on an archaeological site, where, deposit after deposit, the identity of the place is both transmitted and transformed, you see Vercingétorix's personality evolving through time. He is a dangerous enemy and an aggressor in Caesar's text; he is then a victim of Caesar's inflexibility in the course of the Roman period, an invisible man during the Middle Age, a courageous defender of the people and the nation between the Renaissance and the French Revolution, a brave fighter who accepts his defeat during the Second Empire, a patriot defending his land and his people at the time of the French-Prussian War of 1870–71 and the Great War, again a well-intentioned defeated man under the Vichy Regime and the German occupation of France, a *resistant* after 1944 and finally a *Guerrillero* after the time of the decolonization of French Indochina and Algeria ...

Of course, all of these Vercingétorixes – which are, by the way, completely contradictory with each other – have been invented, since it is not at all what the primary historical sources say, which is Caesar's text. But, very curiously, it is not invented from nothing either: it is carefully interpreted from the data contained in Caesar's accounts. So it is plausible. And perhaps more importantly, it may be untrue, regarding the past itself, but it is revealing a powerful truth about the present: when your country is suddenly invaded and conquered – as happened in France in 1871, 1914-1918 or 1940-1945 – you realize what invasion and domination mean, and so you can understand what it also may have meant at the time when Vercingétorix was fighting against the Romans. You are finding new, unexpected meanings within the past. And so, depending on the historical context of the present, this 'reading of the past' takes a peculiar color. It is not at random, indeed, that the interpretation of the Second Empire re-emerges amidst the propaganda of the Vichy Regime: they both tried to justify the legitimacy of the Romanization of Gaul, on one side, and of the 'Germanization' of France on the other.

You said 're-presencing' the past. This is what it is about; Ricoeur called this the 'représentance' of the past – a composite concept bringing together memory and representation.[24] And this is also the approach shared by the German historian Jan Assman, which he coined as *Mnemo-history*.[25] Perhaps what we are painstakingly building is basically some sort of *Mnemo-archaeology*?

In talking together and exchanging our memories, we have seen that we have been following similar lines from different perspectives, meeting the same questions on our way. Maybe it is time now to explore our differences and try to explain how and why they make sense for each of us.

Notes

1. G. Lucas, *The Archaeology of Time* (London and New York: Routledge, 2005).
2. G. Lucas, *An Archaeology of Colonial Identity* (New York: Springer, 2004).
3. G. Lucas, *The Archaeology of Time.*
4. G. Lucas, *Critical Approaches to Fieldwork* (London: Routledge, 2001).
5. L. Olivier (ed.), *Le musée d'Archéologie nationale et les Gaulois, du XIXe au XXIe siècle. (*Saint-Germain-en-Laye: Musée d'Archéologie nationale, 2012); *id.* (ed.). *Autopsie d'une tombe gauloise: La tombe à char de La Gorge-Meillet à Somme-Tourbe (Marne).* Cahiers d'Archéologie nationale, 2. (Saint-Germain-en-Laye: Musée d'Archéologie nationale, 2016).
6. L. Olivier, *Des vestiges* (Mémoire d'Habilitation à Diriger des Recherches (HDR). Paris, Université de Paris-Sorbonne, 2004).
7. L. Olivier, *Le sombre abîme du temps. Mémoire et archéologie* (Paris Le Seuil, 2008); L. Olivier, *The Dark Abyss of Time: Archaeology and Memory* (AltaMira Press, 2011).
8. H. Bergson, *L'évolution créatrice (*Paris: Presses universitaires de France, 1940), Chapter IV; H. Bergson, *Creative Evolution* (tr., Arthur Mitchell, London: Macmillan, 1964).
9. See the key volume S. Holdaway and L. Wandsnider (eds), *Time in Archaeology. Time Perspectivism Revisited* (Salt Lake City: University of Utah Press, 2008).
10. W. Benjamin, *The Arcades Project* (English translation by Howard Eiland and Kevin McLaughlin. Harvard University Press, 1999).
11. A. Warburg, *Bilderatlas Mnemosyne* (London: The Warburg Institute, 2020).
12. H. Focillon, *La vie des Formes* (Paris, Presses universitaires de France, 1943); H. Focillon, *The Life of Forms in Art* (New York: Zone Books, 1992)
13. For example, see G. Lucas, 'Time and the Archaeological Event' *Cambridge Archaeological Journal* 18, no.1 (2008): 59–64; G. Lucas, Time and the archaeological archive. *Rethinking History,* 14, no. 3 (2010): 343–359.
14. C. Hawkes, 1954. Archaeological Theory and Method: some suggestions from the Old World. *American Anthropologist,* 56, no. 2 (1954): 155–168.
15. V. G. Childe, *Social Worlds of Knowledge* (L.T. Hobhouse Memorial Trust Lecture No. 19. Oxford: Oxford University Press, 1949).
16. G. Lucas, 2015. 'Archaeology and Contemporaneity'. *Archaeological Dialogues* 22, no. 1 (2015): 1–15.
17. See G. Lucas, *Writing the Past* (London: Routledge, 2019).
18. G. Lucas, 2010. 'Review of Laurent Olivier, *Le Sombre Abîme du Temps* (Paris: Éditions de Seuil, 2008, 303 pp., pbk, ISBN 978 2 02 096637 5)'. *European Journal of Archaeology* 13, no. 2 (2010): 273–275.
19. L. Olivier, J. Kovacik, 'The Briquetage de la Seille (Lorraine, France): Proto-industrial Salt Production in the European Iron Age', *Antiquity,* 80, no. 309 (2006: 558–566.

20. L. Olivier, 'Iron Age Proto-Industrial Salt Mining in the Seille River Valley (France): Production Methods and Social Organization of Labour', in Danielisova, A. and Fernandez-Götz, M. (eds.): *Persistent Economic Ways of Living. Production, Distribution and Consumption in Late Prehistory and Early History* (Budapest: Archaeolingua, 2015), 69–89.

21. G. Chouquer, *Traité d'archéogéographie. La crise des récits géohistoriques* (Paris: Errance, 2008).

22. I tried to explore this issue in 'La répétition dans les processus archéologiques' *Cliniques, paroles de praticiens en institution*, 14, (2017): 172–186.

23. L. Olivier, *César contre Vercingétorix* (Paris: Belin, 2019).

24. Ricœur Paul, *La mémoire, l'histoire, l'oubli.* Paris, Le Seuil, 2000, 359–369 (Ricoeur, P., 2004. *Memory, History, Forgetting*, Chicago: University of Chicago Press).

25. Assmann Jan, *Moses the Egyptian. The Memory of Egypt in Western Monotheism* (Cambridge University Press, 1997).

Bibliography

Assmann, J. *Moses the Egyptian. The Memory of Egypt in Western Monotheism.* Cambridge: Harvard University Press, 1997.

Benjamin W. *The Arcades Project.* English translation by Howard Eiland and Kevin McLaughlin. Cambridge: Harvard University Press, 1999.

Bergson, H.L. *'évolution créatrice.* Paris: Presses universitaires de France, 1940.

Bergson, H. *Creative Evolution*, tr., Arthur Mitchell, London: Macmillan. 1964.

Childe, V.G. *Social Worlds of Knowledge.* L.T. Hobhouse Memorial Trust Lecture No. 19. Oxford: Oxford University Press, 1949.

Chouquer, G. *Traité d'archéogéographie. La crise des récits géohistoriques.* Paris: Errance, 2008.

Focillon, H. *La vie des Formes.* Paris, Presses universitaires de France, 1943.

Focillon, H. *The Life of Forms in Art.* New York: Zone Books, 1992.

Hawkes, C. 'Archaeological Theory and Method: some suggestions from the Old World'. *American Anthropologist*, 56, no. 2 (1954): 155–168.

Holdaway, S. and L. Wandsnider (eds.) *Time in Archaeology. Time Perspectivism Revisited.* Salt Lake City: University of Utah Press, 2008.

Lucas, G. *Critical Approaches to Fieldwork.* London: Routledge, 2001.

Lucas, G. *An Archaeology of Colonial Identity.* New York: Springer, 2004.

Lucas, G. *The Archaeology of Time.* London and New York: Routledge, 2005.

Lucas, G. 'Time and the Archaeological Event'. *Cambridge Archaeological Journal* 18, no. 1(2008): 59–64.

Lucas, G. 'Review of Laurent Olivier, Le Sombre Abîme du Temps (Paris: Éditions de Seuil, 2008, 303 pp., pbk, ISBN 978 2 02 096637 5)'. *European Journal of Archaeology* 13, no. 2 (2010): 273–275.

Lucas, G. 'Time and the archaeological archive'. *Rethinking History*, 14, no. 3 (2010): 343–359.

Lucas, G. 'Archaeology and Contemporaneity'. *Archaeological Dialogues* 22, no.1 (2015): 1–15.

Lucas, G. *Writing the Past*. London: Routledge, 2019.

Olivier, L. Des vestiges. Mémoire d'Habilitation à Diriger des Recherches (HDR). Paris: Université de Paris-Sorbonne, 2004.

Olivier, L. *Le sombre abîme du temps. Mémoire et archéologie*. Paris: Le Seuil, 2008.

Olivier, L. *The Dark Abyss of Time: Archaeology and Memory*. AltaMira Press, 2011.

Olivier, L. (ed.). *Le musée d'Archéologie nationale et les Gaulois, du XIXe au XXIe siècle*. Saint-Germain-en-Laye: Musée d'Archéologie nationale, 2012.

Olivier, L. 'Iron Age Proto-Industrial Salt Mining in the Seille River Valley (France): Production Methods and Social Organization of Labour', in Danielisova, A. and Fernandez-Götz, M. (eds.), *Persistent Economic Ways of Living. Production, Distribution and Consumption in Late Prehistory and Early History*. Budapest: Archaeolingua 2015, 69–89.

Olivier L. (ed.). *Autopsie d'une tombe gauloise: La tombe à char de La Gorge-Meillet à Somme-Tourbe (Marne)*. Cahiers d'Archéologie nationale, 2. Saint-Germain-en-Laye: Musée d'Archéologie nationale, 2016.

Olivier, L. 'La répétition dans les processus archéologiques', *Cliniques, paroles de praticiens en institution*, 14 (2017): 172–186.

Olivier, L. *César contre Vercingétorix*. Paris: Belin, 2019.

Olivier, L. and J. Kovacik. 'The Briquetage de la Seille (Lorraine, France): Proto-industrial Salt Production in the European Iron Age', *Antiquity*, 80, no. 309 (2006): 558–566.

Ricoeur, P. *La m,moire, lahistoire, laoubli*. Paris: Le Seuil, 2000, 359–369.

Ricoeur, P. *Memory, History, Forgetting*. Chicago: University of Chicago Press, 2004.

3 The past

The issue of the past remaining in the present that was raised in the previous chapter is explored further here, specifically in relation to the larger goals of what it is, that archaeology is trying to do and the kind of stories it writes. The traditional goal of archaeology as 'the reconstruction of the past' is questioned because it presupposes a notion of the past as a time before and separate from the present. Even if archaeology acknowledges that this past only comes to us through the remains that exist in the present, it nonetheless tries to filter out this property of 'remaining' or what Laurent calls 'post-history', to try and get back to some pure past, 'as it once was'. This is the basic premise of formation theory, for example. But there is no such thing as a pure or original past, any more than a pure or original present. Materially, time is always a conjunction of past and present, a polychronic or heterochronic ensemble and the property of 'remaining' and post-history need to be made central, not treated as a methodological constraint. The key problem we try to grapple with in this chapter is how to talk and write about this hybrid mix of past and present, of multiple temporalities in a way that respects such 'remaining'. Can we still tell stories as we used to – stories about the past as if it was a once-lived present? And what about history and historical change? Is conventional, linear history still a viable strategy?

Laurent: As you know, I have been deeply influenced by Walter Benjamin's thought and his rejection of historicism. But several times in our conversation you said that you were not really on the same track since you were 'trying to understand the past in its own terms'. Could you explain what this means for you?

Gavin: It was probably horribly sloppy of me to use a phrase like that: 'the past in its own terms'; it is open to all kinds of interpretation, not least the most vulgar notion that one can understand the past, as it was – rather than through its *transformission* as the archéogeographers say, or through the ideological lens of the present as a postmodernist historian might say. So what did I mean? Perhaps it is best if I approach this back to front, that is, in terms of what I am reacting to. I was uncomfortable with some of the implications of seeing the archaeological remains as contemporary – specifically with the implications of what

DOI: 10.4324/9781003183600-3

the job of archaeology now is, that you were arguing for in *The Dark Abyss of Time*. As you pointed out earlier, one of my criticisms of your book was what do we now do, if we accept all that is implied in the idea of a contemporary past? As I understood you – and you will correct me if I am wrong – you argued that the old goal of archaeology to reconstruct the past, to build stories about what happened in the past, was now in ruins. A mirage or pipe-dream as I believe you called it in a recent publication.[1]

I guess you are now working towards filling out that void – perhaps your book on Vercingétorix is just that. But this mnemo-history you mentioned in the last chapter sounds very much like historiography; a meta-narrative on how we build our histories. In other words, if we accept none of our histories (or archaeologies) have any real basis, they are mere constructs, then the only job left for history and archaeology is to examine the way it (or a society) constructs its stories. Not that this is not an important and worthwhile project, but if archaeology simply becomes archaeography or mnemo-archaeology, it will soon run out of steam – because there will cease to be any production of stories about the past for it to reflect on. Maybe this conflates your approach with a postmodernist position. The idea of transformission does seem to preserve an idea that this is not just all about stories and cultural bias, but also about real, tangible remains. Maybe this is not about replacing history with historiography but blurring the boundary between them. That's ok and there is nothing radical about that. But still we do recognize the distinction and can separate works of historiography from history.

In the case of Vercingétorix, I am sure you are right: writing a history would be pointless as all we have is a handful of sand. But this is an oddly 'historical' subject for an archaeologist to choose – a particular individual. If your subject was 'late Iron Age society in south-eastern France', surely this mere handful of sand has turned into a mountain of archaeological data. I don't see what is so problematic now. I think there are two issues here that we need to distinguish and thus two points at which I would disagree with you on.

The first relates to the possibility of interpreting residues of the past as 'past presents'. Here is where your favourite example of Millie's Camp[2] comes in; this was a paper describing how an archaeologist tried to interpret the residues of a contemporary small group of Native Americans and then compares his interpretation by interviewing its inhabitants. Yes, he got quite a lot wrong – but I always thought it odd how you forget to mention how much he got right. I have never regarded this case study as an argument *against* archaeological interpretation; it is a cautionary tale (as they used to be called), reminding us to be *careful*. And it was precisely because interpretations are often based on 'common sense' rather than systematic research and critical thinking (such as middle range theory was arguing for at the same time this paper came out), that the case against interpreting residues of the past as 'past presents' is not a pipe-dream. It is just hard work.

The second issue, however, is about trying to get back to an original, authentic 'past', an historical bedrock as you call it. This is also a complex issue, because of course there is no original past – any point in the past is itself an amalgam of previous pasts. You have pointed this out as well, and I agree completely. But just because there is no origin does not mean we cannot try and understand the past without always having to refer to how it has come down to us in the present. We need to do this too of course – in some ways, this is what source criticism is. But this should not stop us telling a story, trying to re-presence the past. Recognizing the absence of an origin point just means we think of the past, not as a moment in time, snapshot, but as an *extended present*, a temporally distributed period of time which folds into it, multiple pasts and temporalities, just like you did with the Hochdorf grave. What matters here is not choosing a point in time, but parameters in time – a start and end point, the horizon within which our past extended present takes place. This is all I meant when I suggested we can understand the past in its own terms. That we can still tell stories about what happened back then, though the kind of stories we tell will be dependent on what has persisted from the past into the present. And in telling such stories, we need to be aware of the processes that have modified this persistence (*transformission*). But none of this demands that we must focus solely on these processes. I still think there is a case for archaeology without needing to prefix the mnemo- to it.

But I have said enough – more than enough I suppose to give you cause to respond.

Have I misrepresented you? How would you respond to these points?

Laurent: I believe that we are talking about the same thing, but from different perspectives and maybe approached through different ways of thinking. What you may misrepresent is my position, which is not as assertive as you may think: to tell you the truth, I feel like a blind man in a cave, who is trying to figure out what is lying around. And surely, my use of the English language is not fluent enough to allow me to express such nuances and details that I could evelop in French. But what I keep trying to do, is to build a genuine idea based on our experience of the archaeological record, and not imported from elsewhere – like philosophy, sociology or anthropology …– and this may be a point of disagreement between us. You'll tell me.

So yes, Millie's Camp is indeed one of my favourite examples, since it clearly shows the discrepancy that necessarily occurs between the archaeological interpretation and the historic or ethnographic reality, when you are able compare the 'lived past' that people have experienced or remembered, and the 'archaeological past' that you can reconstruct from its material remains. And here again comes the puzzling question of archaeological time, which, as we have seen, is independent of the so-called 'real time' – the time of people, clocks and history. Yes of course Bonnichsen's team did a good job and they got things right in their interpretation of the place, surely even in the best way that was possible. But this is precisely the reason why they also failed with specific details, since it was clearly unavoidable to do so. They were unable to distinguish between episodic and regular events that took place on the site, since there wasn't any difference in the archaeological record. And they were incapable of sorting the remains that belonged to prior or posterior occupations, since, at this scale of chronological resolution, it was truly invisible. You can't overcome that by being more cautious or careful.

So I don't say that interpreting past occupations like this one at Millie's Camp is a 'pipe-dream' I just say that, when carrying out such kind of work, we have to take into account these unexpected and quite often unnoticeable constraints brought in by archaeological time, which are attached to the materiality of the archaeological record. I believe we both agree about that. The difficult question is how to do that.

When I say that archaeological remains are present residues of an absent past, I just mean this: these vestiges are coming down to us as they are now, already transformed by their post-history as *fossils*. The trouble is that, most of the time, we just ignore what their post-history (their *transformission* if you prefer) has been about. What is nice about Millie's Camp is that the recording of the remains has been so well done that you can use it to set up some sort of a 'mental experiment'.

Table 3.1 Millie's Camp, a virtual experiment in the preservation of the archaeological remains

Preservation of remains	Area 1	Area 2	Area 3	Area 4	Area 5	Area 6	Area 8
Disappears completely	Food Miscellaneous	Clothing **Tobacco** Medication Shelter **Hunting equipment**	Construction materials **Tobacco** Medication Miscellaneous	Food **Tobacco** Miscellaneous	Clothing Food **Tobacco**	Clothing Food **Hunting equipment** Miscellaneous	Food **Cosmetics**
Disappears almost completely	Tobacco	Food			Miscellaneous		
Remains almost completely		Drinks				Drinks	Drinks Miscellaneous
Remains completely	Drinks	**Toys** Cosmetics	**Toys** Cosmetics	Drinks		**Toys** Medication	

In bold: types of remains associated with gender-related or age-related activities.

What would happen if, instead of 1968, we would study this site right now, more than 50 years later, in the 2020's? (Table 3.1)

All the organic components – such as fabric, cardboard, paper, skin or leather ... – would surely have disappeared, reducing what remains by up to 70% in some areas of the site. More durable materials – such as metal, glass or plastic – would remain *in situ*, dramatically transforming the picture of the site. So what would we get? Most of the vestiges on which the interpretation of Millie's Camp was based on would have gone, selectively withdrawing the evidence suggesting male activity, such as tobacco consumption and hunting practices. What would remain would be anecdotal pieces, compared to the original assemblage of garbage abandoned on the site: they would give greater importance to the presence of female and juvenile activity, through pieces of cosmetics and plastic toys for instance. So we would surely interpret this place in a completely different way, perhaps as a place of female feasting and playing with children.

We have known all of this for a long time you would say and I would agree with you. What I am trying to stress with this example is that the archaeological past – as an assemblage of material remains – is unstable and therefore this instability has a direct impact on the way we interpret the lived past which has produced these archaeological remains: we tend to believe that, depending on this loss of material evidence, we would say more or less about this first one, when in fact we would reconstruct different worlds.

But this is just half of what is going on in the 'archaeologization' process, and we all tend to forget the other aspect of this post-history of archaeological evidence – since we don't look at it, focusing our attention on 'the past in its own terms', as you said. As some part of the original information is quickly vanishing over time, another part of what may be called 'secondary information' is accumulating in the course of the 'post-history' of an archaeological past. To put it otherwise, we know far more about the past than the people of the past would have known themselves. Just imagine for a second that you would be able to visit your ancestors who were living let's say three centuries ago: probably you would be unable to fully understand their language, to grasp their habits and figure out their concerns, but surely you would have plenty to observe in their house and their environment – addressing questions which have been shaped by what has happened afterwards. You would *problematize* this past in some unique way, which depends on the posterior 'historization', so to speak, of this moment.

This is, I believe, the very essence of archaeological interpretation, and surely not, as you have put it, some sort of archaeography. This brings me to your second point, which is about this very fundamental question of reaching the past. I have mentioned Benjamin as a major influence on my work, but equally important is also Sigmund Freud. Contrary to most of the commentators of his work – who see in the many comparisons he made of psychic memory with archaeology a simple 'metaphor' – I am convinced that Freud intuitively discovered some major patterns of archaeological time, reading and observing the finds of the archaeologists of his time. It is surprising to see how the evidence of archaeological stratigraphy – that Freud discovered in Schliemann's publication of the excavations at Troy: the profile I showed earlier – contributed to changing Freud's practice and understanding of the new discipline he was building. He obviously realized that stratification is not a simple process of accumulation – one layer *replacing* the previous one – but also of transformation and transmission (again!): the ghost memory of the past is continuously repeated and reinterpreted, always 'at present' in the many following presents of its history; it goes *across* them. This is what I mean when I say that any archaeology is necessarily an archaeology of the present.

I must confess that I have undergone psychoanalysis for some seven years, which has probably made me much more familiar with these strange things. What you realize – to your great surprise – is that you have been 'inventing' your own biography, interpreting events and relationships with people and relatives in a way which was feeding your imaginary construction of yourself and your personal history. You realize that precisely when you begin to discover that what you thought were *facts,* were rather your own interpretation of them, which you made in a particular psychic context. With this psychic context evolving from now on, you discover that there are other interpretations which you have completely missed, of what happened in your past.

This long detour is to stress two important points, I believe:

1. Yes, past events or situations have left durable traces, which bear witness to what they were about; there is no doubt about that.
2. But we only get access to them through an interpretation in the 'afterwards' (in its 'après-coup'), which depends on the present context of this interpretation, which is enlightened by their 'post-history'.

So it doesn't mean, of course, that we have to stop ourselves 'telling stories' about the past: in this matter, we are essentially story-tellers, since this is the only thing we are able to do. But we have to be aware of that: we are not reconstructing the past; we are just, as you put it, *re-presencing* it for ourselves. But we have been talking a lot about *interpreting* the past. If you don't feel like commenting on what I have just said, I would like us to come back to the archaeological evidence and its relationship with the patterns of archaeological time. My position is that we have to change our traditional understanding of archaeology, since it is largely based – as Benjamin would advocate – on some historicist approach of time. *Exchanging ideas with you, I don't feel that you are as demanding as I tend to be. Am I right?*

Gavin: I know what you mean about being a blind man in a cave – I often have that feeling too. I also think we share the same commitment to trying to understand archaeological time from within, rather than simply imposing philosophical ideas from outside. Maybe we just differ in how we approach this; I tend to use philosophy and social theory not as a search for analogs or models to then apply to archaeology, but rather as a foil, to think through archaeological problems or expand my imagination. I suspect our differences in writing and rhetoric are greater than the actual processes of thinking here.

Similarly, perhaps you are right in that I have attributed to you a stronger rejection of the traditional goal of archaeology of telling stories about the past than you actually hold. As you make clear here, you still see this as viable, albeit qualified by an awareness of this post-history. In this sense, we are it seems in agreement. On the other hand, you feel I am not as demanding as you are about changing our traditional understanding of archaeology based on this common understanding, and maybe you are right. Although again, it may depend somewhat on what the demands are and how much change is needed. It is vital we don't talk at cross-purposes here as this has been a recurrent worry of mine, especially when reading your work: how much ground we share and where – if at all – we differ. I think it all comes down to this issue of post-history and also what you mean when you invoke Benjamin's critique of historicism – and what historicism is.

Let me confess now I am not as enamoured of Benjamin as you are. He is very popular I know and what I have read of his work, I have of course enjoyed and found stimulating. But I have always also felt it lacked something, but maybe this says more about me than Benjamin. For example, my understanding of his critique of historicism is that he was arguing against a naïve view of history as a linear succession of events leading somewhere, especially somewhere good. History as progress. It is difficult to be excited by this in 2020 or even in the 1980s when I first read him as it sounds a bit like proclaiming the death of God to a secular age. But I am sure I am missing something else more subtle here; perhaps it is an indictment against seeing any kind of pattern or meaning in history but hopefully you will explain to me better what Benjamin means by historicism. Your example of going back to meet your ancestors three centuries ago was for me, far more stimulating in this regard, although it too I think needs more unpacking as there are a lot of different points in there. For example, I agree that you would problematize this past differently to them, but is this because you came *after* them, you have what historians call hindsight or historical distance – or is it because you are like a person from another tribe or culture, like an anthropologist trying to understand an *alien* society? How do we distinguish historical from cultural alterity or difference? And again, you say we would understand their past *better* than they themselves; is this also due to historical or cultural distance or what?

A lot of questions here but perhaps I can try and bundle them together into two: a) what do you understand by Benjamin's notion of historicism – what does it involve? b) what is it about post-history for you that changes how we tell stories about the past (beyond the obvious, methodological ones around formation processes, source criticism, etc.)?

Laurent: Walter Benjamin is a bizarre and eccentric character, who was not at ease in his body or his time. He was not really a historian, not really a philosopher, not really a writer, but a bit of all three. I mean, to be perfectly clear, that he is not really an authoritative voice for our discipline. I am not enthusiastic either about his aspiration for Marxist revolution and his obsessive attraction for Jewish symbolism. But what I do enjoy is his approach toward the past from, as he says, a *materialist* perspective – which is fundamentally archaeological. This is archaeology invented by an 'outsider', as he considered himself.

The *Arcades project*, that he never achieved, is such a crazy enterprise: studying the cultural spirit of the 19th century from its contemporary material remains, choosing a site which is Paris.[3] Of course, he never saw this as some sort of archaeology of the contemporary past, but rather as some literary wandering in a city full of memories, portraying himself as a stroller, a dreamer. What strikes me in this 'Benjaminian' approach is that it immediately makes time a problem, and therefore history as a challenge – requiring us to reconsider the relationship of history with the time and the past.

This is what Benjamin's critique of historicism is about and it goes far beyond the denunciation of history as progress and historical time as a linear process. In short, Benjamin claims that the past, in order to be truly the past ('in its own terms' as you would say), has to be *recognized* by the present, as some sort of revelation. This is what we do, when you say that, in telling stories about the past, we are importing its presence into our present, 'represencing' the past so to speak. And so this reappearing of the past becomes like a tiger, according to Benjamin: in a bound, he may jump over centuries and even millennia. The past comes back through its many *Nachleben* as Warburg would say.

So we come to the second part of your question, since, as you stress, this is not just about uncovering the past. This is about recognizing it *in the present*. An example immediately comes to my mind, with Camille Jullian, who was the great historian of Gaul at the beginning of the 20th century in France. The First World War had just started when he was teaching at the College de France. During these four years, he was confronted by the bombing of cities, endless trench war, atrocities and misery, in his own country … and he said: I understand now. I understand why, in the historical texts of Antiquity, people have such a special relationship with the ramparts of their cities, which they saw as almost sacred. I understand the shock of invasion, how it troubles the entire society, from the bottom to the top, in many different ways – as it did when Caesar's army invaded Gaul. I hadn't perceived that before the war; in fact, I was unable to get it. But now, I can read those texts in a different way, feeling and being closer to their inner truth.[4]

So you see, this is not just about interpretation, or re-reading the past. It is, as Benjamin argued, about the *meeting* of past and present, in which the aura of the past is revealed within the present and by the present, so to speak. It doesn't change the way we tell stories about the past, but it transforms their identity, I believe. Whatever they consist of – layman novels or scientific works – they are *fictions*, as your personal memories are also fictitious. But fictions in the best way: I mean they carry a powerful truth. They create an effect of veracity, just like when you are reading a very good novel, you feel it's real; it could be the very description of reality. I think that, like writers, this is what we are trying to achieve, as archaeologists or historians, but with different means.

But you are pulling me towards interpretation, when I would like to talk with you about material evidence and this enormous discovery which is, after all, the materiality of time or, to put it otherwise, the question of *time as a property of materiality*. I don't want to appear arrogant, but I have the feeling that you are trying to save the old stuff, which dates back to a period of time when people were unaware of these issues or didn't fully realize what it meant (if this is possible!).

So my question is: how does archaeological time – as this time of material remains – challenge (or not) how we tell stories about the past?

Gavin: Possibly language may be getting in the way again, but I don't see how we can separate interpretation from this issue of the materiality of time. However, since you explicitly raise this question of time as a property of materiality, I will keep my focus there. How does archaeological time challenge (or not) the stories we tell of the past? Well, what is it that we mean by archaeological time? Of course we have in some ways been spending the last two chapters going over this and we more or less agree on a number of things. First, it is defined by the persistence of the past in the present; this is, as you say, Benjamin's starting point for his Arcades project, it underlines Freud's views on memory and the unconscious, and it has become a defining feature for many archaeologists now working on the contemporary past. Second, this persistence is not complete but always partial and transformed as you illustrated with the thought experiment about Millie's Camp. The second point is of course, nothing new, but has been a central element of archaeological methodology, with source criticism and formation theory.

The second point is perhaps also not too important here; because even recognizing this has never stopped archaeologists from telling stories about the past in 'the old way'. It is the first point that is clearly the most important. If the second issue is largely regarded as a methodological problem, the first one might be characterized as more ontological – that is, how does acknowledging that the past can only exist through the present, effect the way we talk about it?

I think the first thing I would say is I am not so sure this is such a recent recognition. I have argued in an earlier paper,[5] that antiquarian and late 19th century archaeologists routinely viewed the archaeological remains in this way because of the close association between archaeological relics and what ethnographers called 'survivals' – that is old customs or habits that have lived on into the present, even though they may have lost all real function (like vestigial organs in biological evolution – our appendix being a classic example). In this way, archaeological time was bound up with a notion of anachrony: stuff that was out of date but still hanging around and as such, gave us clues to our former condition. Over the 20th century, we dropped this idea of course (not least because it was often tainted with evolutionary and racist overtones) and shifted the burden of anachronism from things to thoughts. Now, it is not objects which are guilty of being out of time, it is our ideas or interpretations of the past which are soiled with the sin of presentism – presentism in the sense of interpreting the past through the cultural bias and filters of present-day ideologies. But this came at the expense of making objects belong to a time (the past) and forged a separation of past and present that was much sharper than among antiquarians.

Now, what I think we – and others – are arguing is that it is time to re-situate this temporal disjunction back onto the things. I think this is perhaps what you were getting at when you said I was driving you toward matters of interpretation, whereas you wanted to stay with the materiality of time. But in re-situating time back with things, we are not returning to an antiquarian view which sees the juxtaposition of past and present as one of anachrony, but rather something else. But what is that something else? I admit, I don't know but in general I like to see it reflecting something of the multiple nature of time, a polychronism. But what I do know is that there is a danger this is used simply as a reinforcement of this anxiety around presentism in interpretation. We can never tell stories about the past, so we end up just deconstructing our stories or telling stories about those stories – the points I was making earlier about archaeology as a form of historiography. How do we avoid that? I suppose, in lieu of a clear alternative, I prefer to take the risk and tell stories about the past *as if they were true*. Because right now, I cannot really see even why this recognition that the past only exists through the present, changes anything. At least almost anything.

There is one issue which stands out for me here, which could be my best answer to your original question – and I apologize if I took a long time to get here! That when we talk about re-presencing the past, this is about making the past somehow alive in the present, in a parallel present as when you are reading a novel or watching a movie, you are, while immersed in it, existing in another time, a parallel time. Let's call this 'the archaeological present' when these stories deal with archaeological material and is a cousin of that more familiar term, 'the ethnographic present'. Now in a sense, this kind of account might be called a kind of palaeo-ethnography – albeit of a unique kind, with all the methodological caveats thrown in about imperfect survival. I think this kind of 'story' is not really affected by what we have been saying about archaeological time. However, what has been affected rather is what we might call not the archaeological present but an archaeological history; a narrative that follows a course of events over time (and usually a long time, at least by human scale). The more worrying question is how we write *history* or more accurately, write about *change* in the wake of these recognitions.

Maybe archaeologists have never been good at writing history anyway. Perhaps all we have offered are a series of palaeo-ethnographies, strung together like beads on a necklace (to use Benjamin's metaphor). This isn't history. This is just a sequence of 'past presents', pasted together from which we might abstract some general trends or patterns. At the same time, this also is what archaeological time forces us to do. That an artefact type persists for a certain period of time, until it is succeeded by another; that a certain phase of activity occurs on a site until it is succeeded by another one; that a way of life, an archaeological period like the later Iron Age, lasts in a certain area until it is succeeded by another one. Many of the problems around change – and time – result from adopting this successive view of change, one where all the action is concentrated at the transitions, while in between are just periods of stasis or continuity. In this way, change and continuity are set up as oppositional whereas we need to be better at finding ways to articulate them simultaneously.

But the larger point here is this: one aspect of archaeological time is all about the persistence of the past in the present, of seeing past and present together. But another aspect of archaeological time is very clearly successive or serial. How do we reconcile these two? Well I take the view that actually, the polychronic nature of time implied in the persistence of the past into the present simultaneously offers us a chance to write better history too – as an imbrication of multiple threads or time-lines in such a way that continuity and change operate together. Diagramatically, this is all contained in the time series charts we discussed in chapter 1. However, I think in terms of narrative construction, we have a long way to go to really exploit this. Thus, finally, I think the changes really come down to how we compose our stories and how we use time as an element of this composition to express these things.

Perhaps this seems a rather feeble answer to your question. In fact I don't know how well I have really answered your question, so perhaps I

should just throw the same question now back to you: how does ar-
chaeological time – as this time of material remains –challenge (or not)
how we tell stories about the past?

Laurent: You are throwing the ball back at me, and that's fair: this is
a terribly difficult question – maybe THE question of
archaeology we are facing today. I would approach it from
a slightly different perspective, at once more epistemological
or philosophical. Einstein, among others – like Boltzman –
ushered in a revolution in the definition of time. Today,
we know, since we have experimentally verified what he
calculated, that time doesn't flow at the same speed on the
top of a mountain and at the bottom of a valley, or on a
moving object and at a fixed place. The universe is strongly
heterochronic: everywhere, there is simultaneously an infinity
of different times, all together just right now, in the *Jetzzeit*
would say Benjamin.

And we have found that something similar occurs in the physical
world of archaeology: as the archaeogeographers have shown, landscapes are indeed deeply heterochronic (you said *polychronic*; I wrote
once *multi-temporal*), and so are funerary assemblages (such as the
Hochdorf grave) and anything like the heterogeneous assemblages of
temporalities we used to call sites. As both of us have kept saying, the
past is *in* the present, everywhere.

But, if we take that seriously, we are facing now quite a worrying
problem. Since Einstein, the physicists have never stopped warning us
that what we used to call time doesn't exist in the universe. The only
thing resembling time is *entropy*, but that isn't itself time. Time is an
illusion, wrote Einstein. The physicist Carlo Rovelli has recently
claimed that it is a human perception, which is related to the special
relationship we enjoy, as living species, with entropy.[6]

All archaeological frameworks are based on chronology. Should
we shout out as well: Hey guys, there is no time in the archaeological
past, all of that is just a mirage!? Of course not, but we have to
acknowledge that what we would call *real time* – meaning the time
which has been experienced, or lived by past people and ourselves, as
some ethnographic or historic time – is disconnected from the material time of the archaeological remains. This is what is illustrated
by our pictures of archaeological time 'snaking' up and down the
'line of time', or suddenly accelerating then slowing down, as with
your jars of the Roman period. So I believe we should talk about

Table 3.2 'Old style' and 'New style' archaeological stories (adapted from Olivier 2020)

Old style stories	New style stories
Looking for points of origin	Looking for processes of *emergence*
Identifying events	Identifying *trajectories*
Focusing attention on actions	Focusing attention on *interactions*
Considering materiality as passive	Considering materiality as *active*
Approaching the present as not archaeological	Approaching the *present as archaeological*
Thinking the present as separate from the past	Thinking the *present as containing the past*

human time, on the one hand, and call this ethnographic or historic time, and on the other use *material time* to refer to this strange archaeological time.

So 'where are the stories about the past?' you might ask. They are in between, as a joint product of human time and archaeological time. They are an interpretation, from a human point of view based on what has materially happened, and the word *story* is probably the most convenient for what they basically are. As you mentioned, we are in trouble when we confuse ethnographic time with archaeological time; that is to say human time and material time. It simply doesn't work.

What to do, in this situation? Well, I believe that, depending on if you are a pessimistic person or an optimistic one, there are two different options: the pessimists would say: all of archaeology, as some kind of palaeo-ethnography, is lost and there is nothing to be done anymore. The optimists – and I regard myself one of those – would rather say: this is a unique opportunity to tell new stories or, to put it more precisely, to tell a different *style* of story.

What kind of different style of story? You already said it and so finally I rejoin you here again, but coming from a different direction: *an imbrication of multiple threads or time-lines in such a way that continuity and change operate together.* If I try to summarize the ideas which would lie behind this kind of approach of material time, I get this preliminary list, contrasting this 'new style' of archaeological stories with the 'old' ones (Table 3.2):

Gavin: It is nice to hear you describe yourself as an optimist and also to see you outline your view of how to move forward so explicitly now, as finally I think we are not as far apart as I had thought. Your list of old and new styles is both reassuring and frustrating; reassuring because I can sense some familiar ideas and in some ways, your suggestions for change are things I can see the discipline already doing, such as the shift from origins to emergence or seeing the present as archaeological. But it is also frustrating for the same reason because I am not so sure there is such a sharp break or difference in what we did before. I am not denying the difference, merely that the changes are subtle. But perhaps this is alright; we don't always need a revolution! And after all, am I not the one wishing to preserve something of the old way of doing things?

Notes

1. L. Olivier, 'The Future of Archaeology in the Age of Presentism'. *Journal of Contemporary Archaeology* 6, no.1 (2020): 16–31.
2. R. Bonnichsen, Millie's Camp: An Experiment in Archaeology'. *World Archaeology,* 4, no. 3 (1973): 277–291.
3. W. Benjamin, *The Arcades Project.* (English translation by Howard Eiland and Kevin McLaughlin. Cambridge (MS), Harvard University Press, 1999).
4. C. Jullian, *Au seuil de notre histoire. Leçons faites au Collège de France (Chaire d'Histoire et Antiquités nationales).* (vol. II: 1914–1923, Paris: Boivin, 1931: 38).
5. G. Lucas, 'Evidence of What? On the Possibilities of Archaeology'. In A. Wylie and B. Chapman (eds.), *Material Culture as Evidence.* (London: Routledge, 2014) pp. 311–323. A version of this was actually the paper I gave at the Metz workshop in 2013.
6. C. Rovelli, *The Order of Time* (London: Penguin, 2018).

Bibliography

Benjamin W. *The Arcades Project.* English translation by Howard Eiland and Kevin McLaughlin. Cambridge: Harvard University Press, 1999.

Bonnichsen, R. 'Millie's Camp: An Experiment in Archaeology'. *World Archaeology,* 4, no.3 (1973): 277–291.

Jullian C. *Au seuil de notre histoire. Leçons faites au Collège de France (Chaire d'Histoire et Antiquités nationales).* Volume II. Paris: Boivin, 1931, 1914–1923

Lucas, G. 'Evidence of What? On the Possibilities of Archaeology'. In A. Wylie and B. Chapman (eds.), *Material Culture as Evidence.* London: Routledge, 2014, 311–323.

Olivier, L. 'The Future of Archaeology in the Age of Presentism'. *Journal of Contemporary Archaeology* 6, no.1 (2020): 16–31

Rovelli, C. *The Order of Time.* London: Penguin, 2018.

4 The present

After the difficult exchanges in the last chapter, we here decide to take a different approach to the problem. We focus on the concept of presentism and its relevance for an archaeology of the contemporary. Both of these terms are not to be taken for granted. Presentism, which has many meanings but most recently was used by François Hartog to refer to a specific historical moment or regime of historical consciousness, is here taken apart; instead of being used to define a period, a zeitgeist of how time and history are conceptualized as it is with Hartog, it is taken more widely for an experience of time which foregrounds the present as an immaterial, ephemeral flow. As archaeologists with a focus on materiality however, the present has a much more substantial nature, one that is in fact, dominated by the remains of the past. Connecting this to Giorgio Agamben's writing on the contemporary, we see that the only way to really grasp the present, is through the past. In this sense, an archaeology of the contemporary is, ultimately, one way to frame all theoretical reflection about archaeology and time. As with the concept of presentism, we have to be careful to distinguish this archaeology of the contemporary as a theoretical stance, from archaeologies of the contemporary past as studies of recent and/or current times (i.e. a period definition). As a way to frame theoretical reflection however, Laurent and Gavin come to different conclusions about how this might be situated within the discipline, differences which relate to a divergence in Francophone and Anglophone approaches to theory.

Gavin: One of our first meetings, after many years was at a workshop at Metz in 2014 you co-organized with your colleagues Jean-Pierre Legendre and Jean-Marie Blaising. It was there I was first made aware of Hartog's work on presentism through you, and it has been a dominant theme of your most recent work. *Could you tell me a bit about how you understand the term and how it connects to archaeology?*

Laurent: This term 'Presentism' was coined by the French historian François Hartog in 2003 and it is quite unfortunate, since it may be confused with another very different concept, which has been given the same name.[1] For most people in the Anglo-American world, presentism is an approach to the past, in which you are interpreting the past through a political or ideological lens that is clearly contemporary and would never have existed in the past. In a way, it is a

DOI: 10.4324/9781003183600-4

projection of the present onto the past, which, of course, has been the subject of many critiques.

But what did Hartog mean by this term? He developed this basic observation: when dealing with the past, contemporary historians don't approach it in the same way as their predecessors of the late 19th or early 20th Century. What has changed? Their relationship with time, encompassing past, present and future. We have entered, argues Hartog, a new 'regime of historicity'; meaning that we don't see the present as the natural continuation of the past anymore. Therefore, the present is cut both from past and future and so are we living, in this situation, in some global present – under the *absolute reign of Presentism*, so to speak. When did it change? That's hard to tell, but obviously in the course of the late 20th Century, probably between the late 1980s and the early 1990s. This is basically what Hartog argued.

Is this point just a theoretical concern for European historians, or did Hartog catch 'something which was floating in the air', as one would say in French? Isn't it surprising that, around the same time – the early 1990s – all of us, here and there, were beginning to gravitate around the question of time and materiality? Is it really a coincidence that, around the same period, there was also occurring in anthropology what is now called the 'ontological turn', which is also related to alternative approaches to time? In other words, did Hartog detect some global ontological transformation in the understanding of time within the Human Sciences?

This has been extensively discussed and is the topic of a book that I have recently published with my friend the Estonian historian Marek Tamm, bringing together historians, philosophers and archaeologists.[2] The French historian Jérôme Baschet claimed that Hartog's Presentism is in fact a twofold phenomenon: there is Presentism as *historicity* – as noted by Hartog – but beneath this, there is Presentism as *temporality*: in other words, something happening in the world that is creating the conditions for Hartog's Presentism to appear.[3] What is it? For Baschet, it is obviously the crisis of late financial Capitalism and the separate spread of the Anthropocene. Here again, chronological coincidences are astonishing: if the origins of the Anthropocene are still a matter of debate, there is an agreement, among climatologists, to locate its *'Great Acceleration'* in the course of the second half of the 20th Century, its direct effects becoming increasingly noticeable over these last 30 years, as we know.

So reading Hartog at the time when I invited you to talk about the archaeological present in Metz in 2014, I had quite a similar feeling as Baschet: I thought it was a more global phenomenon than Hartog had observed, and indeed was a matter of temporality rather than just history. Our idea was to bring together many of the people working as archaeologists on the contemporary past and to see what they had to say about this peculiar temporality, compared to the more traditional and conventional approaches toward the archaeological past. But you are right – and I hadn't realized this at that time – the Metz workshop was already oriented towards the question of Hartog's Presentism as a symptom of the temporality of the Anthropocene.

But what about you? How did you approach this 'archaeological present' as temporality?

Gavin: To be honest, it is not really a topic I have engaged much with. I am aware of and have actually used Hartog's ideas a little bit in my writing and talks since 2014, but always with almost the air of a non-believer, or perhaps agnostic would be better. But why is this? I think deep down, I have a skepticism about any theory which argues for the exceptionalism of our times. Even though Hartog's thesis was, in a sense, a sequel to Reinhard Koselleck's earlier theory of regimes of historicity, presentism as the era that follows modernity or *Neuzeit,* modernity was always the original era of temporal exceptionalism, the present as unique. To me presentism is just another inflection of the trope of modernity and in fact reading Hartog through Koselleck, it is clear that the only difference between presentism and modernity is that for Koselleck, the present was still tied to the future (but not the past), whereas under presentism, now the future is cast adrift too. Of course this ignores a lot of the differences between Koselleck and Hartog in the way they analyse these temporal regimes, but the larger point is in both cases, the present takes on the status of an exceptional period in history.

Now when I say I am skeptical of the temporal exceptionalism that underlines concepts like modernity or presentism, this is not to say I don't appreciate the 'difference' of the present. Globalization, the Anthropocene, Finance Capitalism – all these, as you already mentioned, and no doubt more qualities, are certainly unique characteristics of our times. Certainly we are also living in an era where the threat of human extinction is also new. But all this is also only saying that there is something about the contemporary era that is different to preceding eras – but the same applies to any epoch, which means that in a sense, this is simply a question of periodization. And this also then brings me to archaeology and the archaeology of the contemporary past. As you know, this is something I was involved in shaping back in the early 2000s with Victor Buchli,[4] but since then, I have actually done very little work in this area, although my historical archaeology certainly extends into the 20th Century. How did I see it? I suppose at the time, to be honest, I did see it as simply an extension of historical archaeology, as a period designation, as my main concern was to separate it from a purely methodological program, like ethnoarchaeology or middle range theory, which had tainted the earlier attempts to create this field in the 1980s by Rathje and Schiffer. But is the archaeology of the contemporary past simply just another period designation – like Iron Age archaeology or Medieval archaeology? Part of me wants to say no, but I cannot find a reason for making this argument, not without reverting to the exceptionalism of the present. Surely every era has its unique and special qualities, so why make such a big deal over the current one?

Now I know there are other ways of defining the archaeology of the contemporary past – one, being that it is a transformation of archaeology into something more closely resembling heritage studies. But another, is defining it as a period – but as a period like no other, as exceptional. This, for example, is how our colleague Alfredo Gonzáles-Ruibal defines it, and especially in terms of supermodernity and an era of mass destruction.[5] From what I have read of you and what you said earlier, this is also a position you hold. Again, I recognize we are dealing with unique aspects to contemporary times, in terms of scale and speed – these are long acknowledged tropes now of late modernity (here, I am thinking of the work of David Harvey or Paul Virilio[6]), but I also think this is surely a case of elevating the present because this is the era weGonzáles-Ruibal are living in. All of which, comes back to this issue of periodization. That somehow, when you are living in a period, you are almost inclined to see it as exceptional, differently different to anything else before. But is this not just a product of living in these times, rather than having what is called historical distance?

Giorgio Agamben wrote that to truly be contemporary with an epoch, you must be able to live outside it.[7] I think it was even you who first pointed out to me, this short essay by Agamben. Maybe I am misunderstanding Agamben here, but to me, there is something really important here about understanding the nature of contemporaneity and indeed, contemporary archaeology. That it requires we somehow try and position ourselves outside the present – whether before or after, in the past or the future, rather than wallow in some infinite present. If anything, I see Hartog's characterization of presentism as a wake-up call: stop wallowing and imagine!

So, this question you asked about how I view the archaeological present as a temporality; I think it is a red herring. In many ways, the deeper issue here is how is it possible to define a period or time when you are living through it? In some ways, this is an old historical problem, which is why for many historians, contemporary history was an impossibility. I don't agree with this, but the danger is, you go to the other extreme and somehow see it as utterly exceptional. To me, this is where Hartog's presentism seems to lead. Rather, I think we need to dig deeper into this whole question of periodization, contemporaneity and the role a discipline like archaeology has in this context, what kind of interventions it can and should make. And archaeology has always been political, so this is not a question of politics *per se*, but what kind of politics.

But let me come back to you; is this right - do you think we are living in exceptional times and if so, how does that change the archaeology we conduct on the recent and contemporary past?

Laurent: I agree with you about the fact that our present is not necessarily that exceptional, compared to any other period of the past. What is exceptional (for us, as archaeologists) is that we are living in this present period, glued to the contemporary, which makes our historical task impossible. As Agamben has indeed pointed out, we should be able to extract ourselves from the contemporary in order to get the right picture of it. How? – and this is the reason why I suggested you read Agamben: in looking at what is '*inactual*' in the present. What is still present and active in the present, coming from some invisible but powerful past. As Agamben wrote somewhere: *the access to the present is necessarily that of an archaeology.* This is what makes Giorgio Agamben's thought so special for us: just as Michel Foucault was an archaeologist of the Human Sciences, Agamben is building a philosophical archaeology of the present.[8]

So, again, following Agamben, if the present has something special to reveal, this is not about the present itself, but about the *past in the present*. But where has the present gone, in this case? The pure present is what you don't see; it is, according to Agamben, what escapes our observation; it is *transitory, fleeting, contingent*, as Charles Baudelaire wrote about the essence of modernity. And before Agamben, Roland Barthes wrote at the end of his *Mythologies*, that, since the future is basically the overtaking of the present, we can't really see the contemporary.[9] You certainly know this image of time, offered by some

Amerindian cultures: the past is in front of us – exactly like an archaeological site – while the future is what comes from behind our
shoulders, what we can't see.

This looks like a bizarre intellectual game, playing around with
foggy theoretical ideas. But then again, archaeology makes this situation perfectly clear – demonstrating how Agamben is right in his
approach to the present, from an archaeological perspective. In
December 2001 – the last month during which the francs were still in
use, before we turned to euros – I made an archaeological experiment:
I asked as many people I could talk to if I could have a look in their
purses and record the date inscribed on each coin they kept inside. To
put it in archaeological terms, my aim was to date these assemblages
circulating during this month of December 2001, using one of the best
chronological indicators we have in archaeology: coins.[10]

The result I got, from a sample of about 500 coins, was astonishing
(Figure 4.1). There was no coin minted in 2001, meaning that the

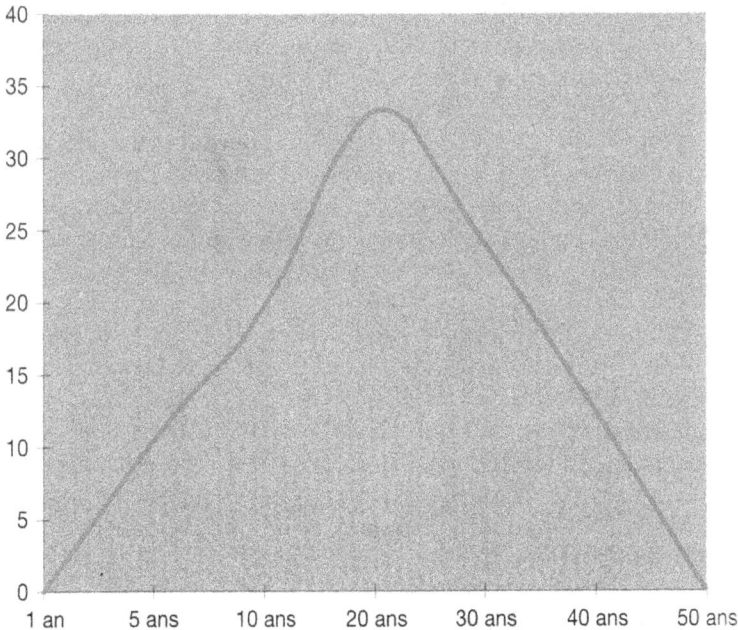

Figure 4.1 Vintage distribution of Francs circulating during the month of
December 2001 (after Olivier, 2001, fig. 9). The values are expressed in percentages.

present, as a period of time, was fully absent from this archaeological record. Instead, the chronological distribution of the coins drew a very nice bell-shaped curve, whose peak was clearly shifted towards the past, by about 20 years. There were even coins minted nearly 50 years ago, which were still in use, every day. Such a picture provides us with a chronological distribution of probability for dating the present (at least this present moment of December 2001): if we would find a random sample of this assemblage of coins (as happens all the time in archaeology), this one would rather date back to an earlier period of time, located several decades ago.

How should we interpret this? We can't really see the present in archaeological materiality; again, we only see the past in the present, which is the basic definition of the contemporary, as Agamben stressed. But then again, where has archaeology gone to, as an event of the present? The archaeological event is what 'comes from behind'; it is pure futurity – and, by the way, this is the reason why it has nothing to do with routine.

I imagine you shaking your head; but look, just try to create an archaeological event in this instant! Everything around you is more or less old – your house, your furniture, your books, your computer…– and even the newspaper that I have got in my mailbox early this morning was printed last night. So dig a hole in the garden and fill it with stuff; or just create a pile of things on your table, in each case making something which has never existed before: you cannot escape rearranging in another way, materials which were already there. This is precisely how Agamben understands the contemporary as some re-presencing of the past. And this is why any archaeology is basically an archaeology of the present, as I have said elsewhere.

But you have drawn me into a discussion which wasn't mine, when I was talking about Hartog and his doomed Presentism. Like Baschet, I am not really interested in Presentism as *historicity* – and I suspect as well, this is the product of some over-interpretation of the recent past; but I am interested in Presentism as *temporality*: I mean what *does* the present, as a condition of archaeological knowledge, do to archaeology, no matter what our present may or may not be as a historical period. *What is your position about that?*

Gavin: I was perhaps not diligent enough in acknowledging your point about the difference between presentism as historicity and presentism as temporality; you are right, my comments about exceptionalism really only bear on the former. But at the same time, I am not sure I recognized the second issue in

Hartog at all – for in many ways what you are talking about in terms of presentism as temporality has nothing to do with Hartog's thesis (at least as I have understood him), so maybe the very term presentism is somewhat misleading. It just adds yet another sense to a term which is already overloaded with alternative meanings, as we have both mentioned earlier. Can we use a different term here? Perhaps, since Agamben seems the more pertinent guide, we should stick with his notion of the contemporary and call this *contemporism*?

Anyway, whatever the label, it is the issue we need to explore here. Your example of the coins is of course a neat one and quite pertinent. I could have suggested we use newspapers instead, and then your curve would probably be more squeezed together and the peak, closer to the 'present' – but this of course would not invalidate your point. All it does is remind us that things have different degrees of ephemerality or durability, that depending on what object you choose, some will 'come closer' to the present than others. But whatever object we select, it will always be past to a degree and of course the present is an ensemble of pre-existing objects and thus saturated with the past. It is like overlying multiple curves from your graph, with multiple peaks, resulting in the present acting as an oscilloscope, the amplitude of the waves presumably being very bunched up closer to the present, and spaced further apart the further back as the persistence of things diminishes.

But what really troubled me about your example is that you talk about the present as simply the sum of the temporality of its elements – coins, newspapers whatever. But the present is surely more than the sum of these things, it is their actual juxtaposition, their *assembling*. The present is this ensemble, not the sum of its parts. So if we were to dig a hole in the ground and bury your coins or any assemblage as you suggest, then the temporality of the present is this act of burial or deposition, not its individual elements. This is the archaeological event; indeed, this is exactly what we study as archaeologists, events like this. And while we may use the 'date' of the elements of this event, i.e. artefacts, to try and date this event, we are fully aware that objects may be old when they went into the ground. We try and triangulate as many different dates as possible to 'date' the event of deposition. Of course we may be wrong, we may be way off – but partly this depends on how precise we want to be (i.e. is our past 'present' of the event reckoned in decades, centuries..?). But you know all this of course, so yes, I am shaking my head – but not in disagreement but in confusion. I don't understand what the point is you are making here unless we are just returning to ground covered in earlier discussion. *Perhaps you can elaborate further on what you mean here.*

Laurent: Please Gavin, don't be afraid about confusion; it could also indicate that something new, but still formless, is emerging from our discussion. So let's be clear first about the vocabulary we are using. For sure, you don't see 'Presentism as Temporality' in Hartog's work, since this lack is exactly what has been criticized by Baschet and other scholars, such as Chris Lorenz.[11] What interests us much more, as archaeologists, is this 'Presentism as Temporality' (which is also the subject of Agamben's discussion), than this rather sterile 'Presentism as Historicity' introduced by Hartog, as you have noted. No doubt Hartog's naming of Presentism was a very bad idea, and I agree with you that we should rather call this peculiar field defined by the primacy of the present simply the *contemporary* – *le contemporain* – as does Agamben himself.

Having said that, I believe we should also differentiate, in our own field of archaeology, between the *archaeology of the contemporary past* – which looks at the recent past historically, e.g. the Industrial Revolution, WWI, WWII, the post-war and post-industrial world – and the *archaeology of the present*, which looks at it temporally. The archaeology of the contemporary past may indeed be considered as some extension of historical archaeology towards some more recent periods of the past – as such as those of the 20th Century – while the archaeology of the present is definitely much more speculative and theoretical. *Would you follow me in this direction?*

Gavin: Yes, I would follow you here – though this question of the archaeology of the present is also precisely what is at stake. But, let's assume – whatever it is – is not the same as the archaeology of the contemporary or recent past. *So what is it?*

Laurent: It is the archaeology of the contemporary, as a temporality. It is approaching the present in a phenomenological perspective, from an archaeological point of view. It is looking at what the present does to archaeology, how it shapes the archaeological record and its interpretation. Millie's Camp is one of the first experiments in this still undeveloped field of the archaeology of the present. My own little work on francs in 2001 is also targeting this shadow area of the archaeological discipline. In contrast to the archaeology of the contemporary past, the archaeology of the present is not focused on any peculiar period of time: it looks at what is happening now, regarding the archaeological materiality.

Again, I believe that we have to adapt our vision of the archaeological record to such a perspective, which is clearly not historicist, and I see why you are still reluctant to do it. But Agamben, as a philosophical archaeologist of the present, may help us, if we read his work carefully enough.

The examples I gave you a few minutes ago – the francs of December 2001, or imagining the creation of an archaeological event just now – are indeed based on our good old concept of *Terminus Post Quem* (*TPQ*). As you pointed out, when mentioning the example of newspapers, the solution we have found to solve this problem is basic: just take the most recent element in your archaeological assemblage, and then you get its closest dating. Fair enough; but, instead of looking at the historicity of this archaeological assemblage, let's look just for a moment at its temporality – as Agamben does with the contemporary.

Basically, an archaeological event could be defined as any material transformation created by some human act or action: right? What Agamben claims is that this act, or this action, is out of our reach, from an archaeological perspective. The burst of the present is what we can't see, since we are just dealing with its material imprint – even if this is only a second later. I don't know how you just made this pile of books and papers on your table. In the Seille Valley, we did not know the course of actions associated with the working of our basins, pits and furnaces, and so we have been unable to reconstruct precisely this technique of salt making. I don't know how the 'prince' of Hochdorf died, and why he was buried in this peculiar way, with nine drink horns at the back of his head.

We used to believe this ignorance was connected to the issue of intentionality – the intentionality of past people – which we can't directly observe, of course, but we may reach, from an archaeological analysis of the remains. But here, Agamben says: - No, it is the present of the past that you cannot reach.

So how should we deal with this problem? This is a terrible question for an archaeologist: that maybe in accepting that what people have been doing in the past, when the past was just the present of their time, is largely unreachable, to repeat Agamben. But this is precisely what the excavations carried out on sites of the contemporary past have repeatedly taught us, over the last 20 years: we don't know what has happened and we are absolutely unable to reconstruct it from the study of the archaeological remains: we have discovered how the Lancaster found at Fléville crashed in 1944 and what happened to the crew from the stories told by the survivors and not from the remains of the wreck, which were mute regarding this issue.[12] Surely, as Agamben suggests, we should rather look at what is inactual in the archaeological record – I mean what is not attached to its peculiar historicity but its transformission. Or, to put it otherwise: in focusing our attention on temporality rather than on historicity. *But tell me: how would you deal with such an archaeology of the present, or the contemporary?*

Gavin: I can see your point that any attempt to capture the present will always be elusive since it can only capture the *imprint* of past presents on future presents; but this is true of any science, from particle physics to the contemporary archaeology of homelessness. I cannot see how this issue has any specific bearing on archaeology. Which makes what you are trying to say even harder to grasp. Thus in regard to your question, I am not sure how to answer this, because everything you are describing sounds to me like the archaeology of the present is a kind of ethno-archaeology, a methodological exercise in what North Americans call middle range research. This was precisely what Victor Buchli and I tried to separate ourselves from when we worked on *Archaeologies of the contemporary past*. It is probably my limited capacity for imagination, but I seem unable think outside these two possibilities: either the archaeology of the present is middle range research or it is a period specialism. But clearly you are trying to draw out a third alternative here, one that is neither of these but something different. Yet Agamben's archaeological philosophy seems too abstract to have any relevance, while the examples you give – Millie's Camp, your coin study – to me, these just seem like examples of middle range theory or ethno-archaeology. *Can you explain to me the difference?*

Laurent: The difference is that they are not based on the same theoretical foundations and it is probably the reason why you find this approach rather difficult to imagine. As you stressed with Victor Buchli in your introduction to the *Archaeologies of the*

Contemporary past, both processual and postprocessual archaeologies shared in common this concern about 'the elucidation of the relation between material culture and human actions or behavior'.[13] To European archaeologists, both theoretical schools felt impregnated with Anglo-American behavioral philosophy, as Paul Courbin noted in a very nasty book about the *New Archaeology*.[14]

I was very angry at him when I read this book for the first time, but re-reading it today, I must confess Courbin was right on many points. Perhaps the 'turn' of the 1990s that we have evoked regarding the importance of time was also that of the loss of our illusions. Processual and post-processual archaeologies were Anglo-American illusions: processualists have never established any archaeological 'law', as they loudly proclaimed to achieve, and postprocessualists never 'elucidated' anything about the behavior of past people. Middle range research, as well, never produced any 'theory', if this word still bears a meaning. This ambitious research program, which had been set up in the early 1960s as a war machine against 'traditional' European archaeology, has collapsed under its own weight.

And it was ideological too, since you, our old English neighbors, our old cousins and rivals, you chose to follow the Americans, thinking you were speaking the same language, imagining you were sharing the same interests and values. *Brexit* is the contemporary equivalent for the long-standing illusion of this assumption in the archaeological field, already more than 50 years before Boris Johnson came to power.

To tell you the truth, this made us sad and sorry. It was sad, when you knew how foundational the role of British Prehistory had been in the development of French Prehistory at the end of the 19th Century. And it was also distressing, since it was so obvious that the arrogance of these self-proclaimed *new* or *post* archaeologies were in fact the voice of this triumphant Post-war American economic domination, so certain in its conviction of being right on any occasion, especially when it was doing wrong. Surely Trump's election has finally helped to pull down the seductive and entertaining mask that America has been wearing for too long a time. As James Baldwin wrote about his fellow Americans: We are cruelly trapped between what we would like to be and what we actually are. We cannot possibly begin to become what we would like to be until we ask ourselves exactly why the lives we live on this continent are mainly so empty, so tame, and lonely.[15]

This American country has indeed been built on land theft and the genocidal erasure of indigenous people, together with slavery and white supremacism, as the American historian Roxanne Dunbar-Ortiz recently wrote.[16] Trump's election was not some unfortunate accident; it reveals America's deep historical identity. I believe it is time to open our eyes now: we cannot be terrified by what happens in America – since the way people are treated there is truly terrifying – and, at the same time, find its archaeology cool and constructive. This is not only a schizophrenic attitude; to be honest, it is also quite a bit obscene.

Even the concept of ethno-archaeology itself, whose practice has developed from the 1970s in American archaeology, is problematic. It is based on an asymmetric sharing of mankind, established on the exclusion of the 'Others' – the non-whites in fact – from the privilege of creating history:[17] we have, ourselves, an 'archaeology of us', of our contemporary past, when these poor 'Others' don't. They are just the subject of our ethno-archaeology, whose aim is to exploit their 'primitive' behavior in order to interpret our own remote past, when we were still at this archaic state of development, a state that those present 'Others' have been unable to overcome, remaining stuck in our vanished Prehistory. This is what the ethno-archaeological discourse is basically about.

So you ask what is the archaeology of the present about, compared to ethno-archaeology or middle range theory? Precisely what these approaches aren't: *a critical tool for archaeology*.

I am afraid there is a misunderstanding between us – one caused by the difference between the Anglo-American research approach and the French one – which is worming its way into our discussion. When invited to give a talk in the States, I am always surprised to discover how insistent people are to convert what I have said into a *system,* how avid they are to get something to *believe* in. And I know that I am going to deeply disappoint them, since I am not bringing any new faith; I am just proposing a *critique*.

You read Ricoeur, Deleuze, Derrida and many other French thinkers. What all these people share in common is this: they don't aim to build a system – or what you may call a *theory* – they just develop a critique: a critique of this very thinking in terms of systems. They just tell their readers: 'Hey, look, from the point of view where I am standing now, one may see this theoretical object, which looks so perfectly defined, in quite a different way, and this is interesting, for a lot of unexpected reasons'. This is why transforming Foucault's thought into a theoretical system, for instance – or any other of these 'French thinkers' – is the most enormous nonsense one may do.

So, like these people, I am trying to develop a critique of archaeology, and this is indeed the limit of what I do. But *how* might this archaeology of the present may be a critical tool, you would ask? What is unique about the present is that the producers of archaeological materials are among us – no matter whether they are 'Us' or some 'Others'. It helps us to measure not the similarity but the difference between what we see, when people are creating archaeological stuff, and what we imagine, when we are excavating archaeological sites. It should provide us with some sort of a parapet, restraining over-interpretation and ideological extrapolation. This is how I see a decent archaeology of the present: as a weapon against any intimidating form of discourse in archaeology – a counter-power so to speak.

But you keeping asking me questions and I keep answering, when you say very little about your own view. You see where I stand: I am a European archaeologist, trying to maintain an independent way of thinking, which is inevitably deeply influenced by my French in-heritance. *What about you? Where are you in relation to Anglo-American and European research programs?*

Gavin: Where do I stand? Well that is a good question but before I answer you, I want to just go back over a few things you said (there, you see I am already trying to avoid the issue!).

First, I think you are too damning of the fallout from Anglo-American theory; yes, New Archaeology had some lofty ambitions which it never quite attained, which is why it softened into processualism. And maybe postprocessualism never quite recovered 'past minds and meanings', but it too opened up vistas never previously considered. I don't see them as failures at all, nor illusions – if anything, they helped to strip away many of our illusions. Indeed, critique was just as much a part of their program as systemic, theory building. The French certainly don't have the monopoly on critique! I will come back to this in a moment though.

Regarding ethno-archaeology and the archaeology of the present; again, I think you portray ethno-archaeology as way too colonialist; of course there is a dimension of colonialism to it, but to claim it is the appropriation of the present of the Other for the purpose of eluci-dating the past of Us, is surely very selective. Ethno-archaeology is used just as much to elucidate the prehistory of Africa or North America as it is the Neolithic of Europe. And this ignores the im-portant discourses around ethnohistoric analogy and folk history or what they call the Direct Historical Approach in the U.S. If there is any appropriation, it is rather the general one of archaeology as a western discourse appropriating the past (and present) of Others for its own ends under the guise of the True or Scientific version of history.

Anyway, these issues are tangential to your main point, but I felt the need, nonetheless, to counter them. But as to your main point: you describe the archaeology of the present as the means to 'measure not the similarity but the difference between what we see, when people are creating archaeological stuff, and what we imagine, when we are excavating archaeological sites'. Well to me, this just reads, again, like a definition of middle range theory. But I don't want to be obtuse so I am going to try and understand this in terms of what else you have said, specifically this issue of critique. Part of the problem relates to how I am using the term middle range theory and indeed, theory in general – which is a point you also raise so maybe this is what I need to address next.

You are right about one thing – perhaps especially in the U.S. (and to a lesser extent in Britain), archaeologists expect theory to offer some kind of system or paradigm: like a tool for how to address the many interpretive problems we face when encountering archaeological remains. You say that all you are trying to do is offer critique and this results in all kinds of misunderstandings and false expectations. I think there is definitely an important point here about theory in general and how it is viewed by Anglo-American archaeologists and many European ones; and I agree that the paradigm or system model is very problematic, even if it does occasionally seem very pragmatic. (There probably is a connection here to the American philosophy of pragmatism, but probably not in the obvious way. But that's another matter.) Yet for an Anglo-American ear (or my ear at least!), critique is always just *half* the story; critique is vital and has been a part of Anglo-American archaeology all along, especially political critique which was central to post-processualism and its connection to feminism and postcolonialism. But critique is like saying – 'hey, I just point out the problem, it's not my job to find a solution!' We need to build on critique to find ways to address disciplinary problems, to move discourse forward. But I am guessing your conception of critique might include a broader remit, so hopefully you will expand on this.

Moreover, that's why I find Millie's Camp such a strange example for you to stick with; it was a cautionary tale, a critique, reminding us of where we go wrong. I see it as a precursor to middle range theory which tried to pick up the warnings offered by cases like Millie's Camp and turn them into something that we can use – to help us find solutions, not just point out the problems. Now for sure Middle Range Theory got way too ahead of itself, believing it could come up with the Rosetta stone for material traces; but in the attempt, we learnt an awful lot and still are. I don't see MRT as pointless, rather we just need to accept it for what it really is: old fashioned analogy, despite attempts to make it otherwise. It is never going to give us laws or rules, but it does give us ideas. Of course maybe we should not call my version of this MRT, as the term conjures up very specific processualist agendas, but let's not worry about that here. But the point is, we need to always find a balance between theory as critique which offers no solutions, and theory as a pure tool or system which pretends to solve all our problems.

So let me finally try and answer your question and tell you where I stand. As already hinted, I find it hard to think of the archaeology of the present in terms other than *either* a period designation *or* a kind of middle range theory (which I take in very broad terms as a context good to think with like old-fashioned analogy, not necessarily as a rule-seeking system as originally devised under processualism). I suspect this second definition is probably much closer to yours. At the same time, I feel like this discussion had really moved away from being about an archaeology of the present to simply, being about theory in general. Somewhere along the way, I feel the issue of temporality has been lost. Because it seems to me, what we are really talking about here is simply how our experience of living, right here, right now, should somehow be connected to what it is we are doing when we try and understand archaeological remains. To me, this whole issue is more about the general fact that as an archaeologist studying what remains of the past, we are situated in the present which is temporal yes, but also political, cultural, material, etc. All of which have been a key part of (Anglo-American) theory for decades. Why is temporality so crucial here?

So as to your question: where am I, in relation to Anglo-American and European research? I was raised in one, but with a deep desire to re-connect to the latter, which I think I am doing, especially through thinking about the role of theory. This is something we Anglo-Americans probably all have to do in the wake of what has been called the end of paradigms as signalled by the 2019 EAA conference in Bern. For me, I am certainly closer to the Anglo-American tradition, but I also see it as in great need of reconstruction and in part, by talking more closely *with* (not at!) my European colleagues – as we are doing here. I agree with you that theory cannot be thought of as a system or tool to apply to a set of data; it is really not helpful to think of it like this and doing so has generated some of the worst kind of garbage and nonsense but also produced a lot of failed expectations. It's not all bad though either – it has broadened horizons and in fact in some ways, it has worked best precisely when it *is* critique. But occasionally, in the right hands it has also created some very insightful work. But really, what we need is to think of theory less as a tool, more as a space for thinking, part of which is critique, part of which may lead to novel ways of interpreting or engaging with archaeological remains. Theory remains pragmatic, without being instrumental. What matters is the dialogue we have, with others and with our material. But I have said enough now. *Perhaps you can address some of the questions I raised here – and if you are not happy with my response to your question, by all means press me further!*

Laurent: This exchange of ideas between us is fascinating – and I hope it is for our readers too: it not only reveals us to each other, but it reveals us to ourselves as well. You know this silly joke which says: 'Hell is when the police are German, the lovers Swiss, the mechanics French, the chefs British and it is all organized by Italians'. Of course, it is a stupid cliché, but there is a bit of truth in it and this is why it is funny. We French are not good, as a nation, in mechanics or in building systems and theories in the field of the Human sciences. Guess who are? The Germans. We are at our best when it is a matter of fighting against any kind of dominant discourse. We are creative and imaginative, but we are also messy, sometimes superficial, and inconstant. Not all of us, naturally, but this is a global tendency among us. As English, you are creative and imaginative too, but also pragmatic and more rigorous than we tend to be. Your weakness is intolerance, a defect you have in common with Germans and Americans: you tend to consider that there is only a right way to do something and all the others are wrong. And this is why you are attracted to systems and theories. Not you personally of course, but this is as well a general cultural trait among Anglo-American people.

Processual and postprocessual archaeologies were Anglo-American offensives against traditional European archaeology. It was fair, because continental archaeology had been deeply infected by fascism and Nazism during the 1930s and 1940s.[18] And German archaeologists, who had been ideologically working for the Nazi regime, had a strong influence on the rebuilding of French archaeology after WW2, up to the end of the 1980s. This tacit inheritance was one of the reasons that I came to Cambridge: to breathe some fresh air.

But then what choice did I have? One option was to leave completely and try to get closer to the heart of Anglo-American archaeology; I mean the US. This is what many of our colleagues did such as Michael Shanks, Ian Hodder or Sander van der Leeuw. But I knew I was never going to become an American, remaining forever what you call an alien – which is, in the English language, the same word used to name extra-terrestrial beings! The other option was to go back home and rediscover there what it was I had tried to escape from. This is what I finally chose to do. Not only because I already had a job in France waiting for me but also because I thought – and I still sincerely do – that we are indeed different but moreover we are complementary. If we could trust each other, the French, the British and the Germans, and work together like brothers, we could achieve great things. This is the reason why I came back, but I maintained the dialogue with my Anglo-American friends and colleagues: yourself in Reykjavik, Matthew Reilly and Chris Witmore in the US, Chris Gosden at Oxford ... and many others.

So the context is different and has shaped the direction I have followed. Surely, it is no coincidence that my intellectual influences are directly derived from the German-Jewish thinkers of the pre-Nazi period: Sigmund Freud, Walter Benjamin, Aby Warburg. This wasn't on purpose but this is the way it happened: in fact, I realize that I am just trying to heal the wound which had been inflicted by fascism and Nazism on the European intellectual tradition. And I understand this could not be your primary concern. You belong to a different history.

But we know each other well enough, to be able to talk frankly to each other, without fear of hurting each other: in the 1990s, it was already clear, from an outsider's point of view, that postprocessual archaeology wasn't going anywhere. Similarly, you don't need to have second sight to see actually that the post-war Anglo-American domination is over and has already begun to crumble. Brexit is a British suicide. So what to do? What is going to come next?

Notes

1. F. Hartog, *Régimes d'historicité. Présentisme et expériences du temps* (Paris: Le Seuil, 2003); F. Hartog, *Regimes of Historicity. Presentism and the Experience of Time* (New York: Columbia University Press, 2016).
2. M. Tamm and L. Olivier, *Rethinking Historical Time. New approaches to Presentism* (London & New York: Bloomsbury, 2019).
3. J. Baschet, *Défaire la tyrannie du présent. Temporalités émergentes et futurs inédits* (Paris: La Découverte, 2018).

4. V. Buchli, V. & G. Lucas (eds.), *Archaeologies of the Contemporary Past* (London: Routledge, 2001).
5. A. Gonzáles-Ruibal, A Time to Destroy. An Archaeology of Supermodernity. *Current Anthropology* 49, no. 2, (2008): 247–79; A. Gonzáles-Ruibal, *An Archaeology of the Contemporary Era* (London: Routledge, 2019).
6. D. Harvey, *The Condition of Postmodernity. An Enquiry into the Origins of Cultural Change* (Oxford: Blackwell, 1990); P. Virilio, *Negative Horizon. An Essay on Dromoscopy* (London: Continuum, 2005).
7. G. Agamben, G. 'What Is the Contemporary?' In G. Agamben *What Is an Apparatus? And Other Essays* (Stanford: Stanford University Press, 2009) pp. 39–54.
8. Michel Foucault, *Les Mots et les Choses. Une archéologie des Sciences humaines* (Paris: Gallimard, 1966); M. Foucault, *The Order of Things: an archaeology of the human sciences* (New York: Vintage, 1973); Adney Jdey and François Nault (eds.), *Giorgio Agamben. Une archéologie du présent* (Paris: Le Bord de l'Eau, 2014).
9. R. Barthes, *Mythologies* (Paris: Le Seuil, 1957), pp. 232–233; R. Barthes, *Mythologies* (London: Vintage, 2009)
10. Not a very original idea! It was reproducing, in a different way, what I had done with miner's lamp for my PhD. This experiment has been published in L. Olivier, 'Temps de l'histoire et temporalités des matériaux archéologiques: à propos de la nature chronologique des vestiges matériels', *Antiquités nationales*, 33, (2001): 189–201.
11. C. Lorenz, "Out of Time? Some Critical Reflexions on François Hartog's Presentism", in Tamm M. & Olivier L. (eds.), *Rethinking Historical Time. News Approaches to Presentism* (London & New York: Bloomsbury, 2019), 23–42.
12. Jean-Pierre Legendre, 'Archaeology of World War 2. The Lancaster bomber of Fléville (Meurthe-et-Moselle, France)', in V. Buchli and G. Lucas, *Archaeologies of the Contemporary Past* (London & New York, Routledge, 2001), 126–137.
13. Victor Buchli and Gavin Lucas, 'The absent Past. Archaeologies of the contemporary past', in V. Buchli and G. Lucas, *Archaeologies of the Contemporary Past* (London & New York, Routledge, 2001), 5.
14. Paul Courbin, *Qu'est-ce que l'archéologie? Essai sur la nature de la recherche archéologique* (Paris: Payot, 1982), 34; P. Courbin, *What Is Archaeology? An essay on the nature of archaeological research* (Chicago: Chicago University Press, 1988).
15. J. Baldwin, *I Am Not Your Negro* (Compiled and edited by Raoul Peck. London, Penguin Books, 2017), 87.
16. R. Dunbar-Ortiz, *An Indigenous People's History of the United States* (Boston, Beacon Press, 2014).
17. As has pointed out Johannes Fabian in his *Time and the Other. How Anthropology Makes Its Object* (New York: Columbia University Press, 1983).
18. See L. Olivier, *Nos ancêtres les Germains. Les archéologues français et allemand au service du nazisme* (Paris: Tallandier, 2012); also J-P. Legendre & L. Olivier, 'Les braises sous la cendre: la survie de l'archéologie nazie après 1945', in les usages du passé. *Cahiers d'Histoire immédiate*, 43, (2013): 81–112.

Bibliography

Agamben, G. 'What is the Contemporary?' In G. Agamben *What Is an appa-ratus? And other essays*. Stanford: Stanford University Press, 2009, pp.39–54.

Baldwin J. *I Am Not Your Negro*. Compiled and edited by Raoul Peck. London: Penguin Books, 2017.

Barthes, R. *Mythologies*. Paris: Le Seuil, 1957.

Barthes, R. *Mythologies*. London: Vintage, 2009.

Baschet, J. *Défaire la tyrannie du présent. Temporalités émergentes et futurs inédits*. Paris: La Découverte, 2018.

Buchli V. and G. Lucas 'The absent present: archaeologies of the con-temporary past', in Buchli V. and Lucas G. (eds.), *Archaeologies of the Contemporary Past*. London & New York, Routledge, 2001, p. 3–18.

Buchli, V. and G. Lucas (eds.) *Archaeologies of the Contemporary Past*. London: Routledge, 2001.

Courbin, P. *Qu'est-ce que l'archéologie? Essai sur la nature de la recherche archéologique*. Paris: Payot, 1982.

Courbin, P. *What Is Archaeology? An Essay on the Nature of Archaeological Research*. Chicago: Chicago University Press, 1988.

Dunbar-Ortiz, R. *An Indigenous People's History of the United States*. Boston, Beacon Press, 2014.

Fabian, J. *Time and the Other. How Anthropology Makes Its Object*. New York: Columbia University Press, 1983.

Foucault, M. *Les Mots et les Choses. Une archéologie des Sciences humaines*. Paris: Gallimard, 1966.

Foucault, M. *The Order of Things: An Archaeology of the Human Sciences*. New York: Vintage, 1973.

Gonzáles-Ruibal, A. 'A Time to Destroy. An Archaeology of Supermodernity'. *Current Anthropology* 49, no. 2, (2008): 247–279.

Gonzáles-Ruibal, A. *An Archaeology of the Contemporary Era*. London: Routledge, 2019.

Hartog, F. *Régimes d'historicité. Présentisme et expériences du temps*. Paris: Le Seuil, 2003.

Hartog, F. *Regimes of Historicity. Presentism and the Experience of Time*. New York: Columbia University Press, 2016.

Harvey, D. *The Condition of Postmodernity. An Enquiry into the Origins of Cultural Change*. Oxford: Blackwell, 1990.

Jdey, A. and Nault, F. (eds.) *Giorgio Agamben. Une archéologie du présent*. Paris: Le Bord de l'Eau, 2014.

Legendre, J-P. 'Archaeology of World War 2. The Lancaster bomber of Fléville (Meurthe-et-Moselle, France)', in Buchli V. and Lucas G. (eds), *Archaeologies of the Contemporary Past*. London & New York: Routledge, 2001, pp. 126–137.

Legendre, J-P. and Olivier, L. 'Les braises sous la cendre: la survie de l'archéologie nazie après 1945' *Cahiers d'Histoire immédiate* 43 (2013): 81–112.

Lorenz, C. 'Out of Time? Some Critical Reflexions on François Hartog's Presentism', in Tamm M. & Olivier L. (eds.), *Rethinking Historical Time. News Approaches to Presentism*. London & New York: Bloomsbury, 2019, pp. 23–42.

Olivier, L. 'Temps de l'histoire et temporalités des matériaux archéologiques: à propos de la nature chronologique des vestiges matériels', *Antiquités nationales* 33 (2001): 189–201.

Olivier, L. *Nos ancêtres les Germains. Les archéologues français et allemand au service du nazisme*. Paris: Tallandier, 2012.

Tamm, M. and Olivier, L. *Rethinking Historical Time. New approaches to Presentism*. London & New York: Bloomsbury, 2019.

Virilio, P. *Negative Horizon. An Essay on Dromoscopy*. London: Continuum, 2005 [1984].

5 The future

While in the last chapter we tried to avoid thinking about the present or contemporary as an historical period, one of the biggest issues that has emerged within academia in the last decade has been the concept of the Anthropocene as a defining feature of contemporary times. The Anthropocene is important because it connects the past to the future through the phenomenon of human impact at a planetary scale; it forces us to see how past actions are shaping future possibilities. In this chapter, we devote most of our discussion to thinking about the implications of the Anthropocene for archaeology. For scholars wanting to research the archaeology of the Anthropocene, especially of the last century, the scale and nature of the archaeological record test our current methodologies and approaches. How do you study vast, hybrid formations like the Great Pacific Garbage Patch, a gyre of marine debris (composed mostly of micro-plastics) in the northern Pacific which covers an area of hundreds of thousands of kilometres? Such 'hyperobjects' challenge both tradi-tional notions of scale but also the separation of human and earth his-tory. We each approach this problem from slightly different angles; for Laurent, the issue is about the hybrid nature of these materialities, their conflation of human and natural processes; for Gavin, the issue is about scale, specifically the language of scale as it is applied to time. For both of us though, it is clear that new vocabularies, new ways of thinking about these vast materialities are needed, and this is something to which archaeology can make a great contribution.

Laurent: We have been talking extensively about the past and present, which are our main topics as archaeologists, for reasons given in our discussions of these previous pages. *But what about the future? I mean how could archaeology provide some useful conceptual tools for grasping the transformations of the future? And how may our understanding of time contribute to this?*

Gavin: These are big, tough questions and I imagine we will spend the rest of this chapter just scratching their surface. But we need to start somewhere I suppose so I will begin at an obvious place. That even though archaeologists are ostensibly focused on re-presencing the past, it is also quite clear that such acts are intended to reverberate into the future. This takes many forms, from simply the collection of artefacts and archives which are intended for

DOI: 10.4324/9781003183600-5

preservation into an undefined period of the future to the impact we hope our work will make on future scholars and the discipline itself. All of which suggests to me that a key issue here which ties the past and future together is one of inheritance, of passing on or passing down of things from the past, to the future. And so the relation to time now also becomes clearer: to what extent does this 'passing on' relate to the passage of time?

The future of course can be conceived in many ways but I do think, as archaeologists, it is in this relation of the past to the future that we have something most to contribute. In the age of the Anthropocene, there is a lot of talk now of the role archaeology can play, by digging into our past as a source of gathering alternate ways of living, of coping with environmental change, forms of resilience and so on. Treating the past as a library of ideas, life-solutions which may help us plan for unexpected futures. This is all good and well, but it is also a very old idea, history as *magister vitæ*, a life instructor from which one can obtain models or exemplars. To learn from past mistakes and such like. But what is missing here is something more concrete, more material, more temporal which the idea of inheritance encompasses. Because inheritance as a material process is where it all happens; that arguably, the very passage of time is constituted by the multifarious processes of 'passing on'. Some of this is being addressed now by research such as the heritage futures project run by Rodney Harrison, Cornelius Holtorf and others, exploring heritage and conservation as a future-assembling practice.[1] Seed banks, nuclear waste repositories and so on, are really good examples of this materiality of inheritance. But then so are governmental and institutional structures for the preservation of wealth; what really struck me when I read Thomas Piketty's book *Capital* a few years ago was how inheritance really played the central role in the creation of wealth inequality.[2] It is by digging into inheritance structures that I think archaeologists can offer the most useful contributions to both understanding and transforming our future.

But since you asked the question, you must have your own response too. What is that?

Laurent: I must say this looks like a weird question – wondering about the future – since archaeology is supposed to be primarily concerned with the traces of the past. But as you say, working as an archaeologist is a transmission job which targets the future: we do our best to pass on the present archaeological heritage, as well as the knowledge which has been accumulated about it, to the next generation.

But more deeply, as you suggest, any material creation is a message addressed to the future. People don't expect their parents' grave to be wiped out when they die themselves for instance, and this is the reason why they maintain family vaults. So our present material creations will become the archaeological heritage of the future: our gas stations, our airports, our supermarkets ... Well; this is interesting, as one says in English – meaning why not, but it is in fact not such an exciting idea!

Heritage futures projects are rather a dull idea if they are conceived within the traditional perspective of historicity: I mean 'cutting history into slices', as the historian Jacques Le Goff wrote;[3] that is to say, merely considering these creations of our present material culture as the next coming historical slice. You asked why temporality is so crucial for the apprehension of the present in Agamben's sense (I mean the burst of the future in our present time)? Precisely for this reason: because it is lacking any archaeological interest if it wasn't.

This brings us back to materiality again. If we consider that archaeology is basically the study of material transformation created by human activity, therefore our present time is the most archaeological that has ever existed. Our material impact on the landscape, the diversity and number of artefacts we daily produce, are far greater than those of any other period of human history. Similarly, the durability of our constructions and products is also beyond any scale, compared to those of the past; just think about nuclear waste, for instance, some of which is going to remain highly radioactive for hundreds of millennia, or even millions of years.

Some people call this unprecedented situation the *Anthropocene*. What is new is not the nature of the human impact, it's rather its *scale*. The question is not about knowing if the Anthropocene is, or is not, a new geological era – or a new archaeological age. It is not either about dating its beginning or wondering if this is a fruitful concept, or the best labelling for what has been accelerating since the Post-War period. It is to assess what it does to archaeology.

And the impact of the so-called *Great Acceleration* of the Anthropocene on the archaeological discipline is huge. The development of preventative archaeology – which is called *commercial archaeology* in the Anglo-American world – is a direct effect of the pressure of the Anthropocene on the inhabited landscape. We dig where development projects are going to erase the material memory of the places they target, excavating huge surfaces, some of them covering hundreds of hectares. We don't just study archaeological sites anymore but mainly archaeological landscapes. And we have to dig everything which is threatened by these development projects – even those vestiges of the most recent historical periods. In Continental Europe – where remains of the two World Wars are highly concentrated – the development of the archaeology of the contemporary past is directly related to such preventative excavations. We may say this is an indirect effect of the Anthropocene on the practice of archaeology.

But I don't feel like dwelling too much on this matter so I would rather like to ask you how you see this question of the impact of the Anthropocene on archaeology?

Gavin: Well, as you so eloquently pointed out, the massive rise of commercial or development-led archaeology is a direct product of the new scale of human intervention on the planet that has escalated over the 20th and 21st centuries. Historically, this kind of archaeology has often been linked to post-WW2 urban reconstruction in the wake of bombed out cities, but in the USA for example, it began with the TVA and WPA large-scale government work programs in the 1930s which suggests a more general motive, one linking large-scale construction with large-scale conservation. The immediate impact to this discipline has of course been a rise in employment for archaeologists, and a rise in archaeological data; not just more of it, but new types of data. Regional or period-based textbooks are almost out of date as soon as they are published; who dares write a textbook for Iron Age France or Britain today knowing the rate at which new sites and data are excavated each year? Of course someone usually does, but these days – at least in the English-speaking world, such textbooks resemble more a series of thematic essays, handbooks, because – irony of ironies – theory now changes more slowly than new data or evidence.

Still, all I am doing here is repeating or elaborating upon the same point you just made. Do I see anything else about this phenomenon we call the Anthropocene that has an impact on archaeology? Well, since time is ostensibly our main matter of concern in these discussions, let me bring us back to that. I recently read an interesting paper by one of the more perceptive commentators on the Anthropocene, Dipesh Chakrabarty who talked about the deep schism in this discourse around the geological time scales of change and the human time scales of political action and response.[4] It is as if these two discourses run side by side without being aware of the deep incompatibility in their temporal register. What makes this particularly interesting for archaeology is that it operates under the same illusion. It has always lauded its attachment to deep time or the long term, yet at the same time, in a similar way, also cleaved to its role as the study of human life. And how has archaeology tried to resolve this paradox for itself? Of course many of us just ignore it. Some only focus on long-term processes, others on the scale of lived experiences. But some do try and mediate these scales, whether drawing on Braudel (who didn't actually mediate them at all) or some other means.[5] But frankly, I have not really been convinced by any of these attempts. Which makes me suspicious of the concept of scale in the first place.

All of which now seem to bring me to a place where, instead of agreeing with your diagnoses about the impact of the Anthropocene – it's all about scale – I find myself becoming suspicious of it. That focusing on scale will just increase our sense of helplessness and inability to resolve this paradox outlined by Chakrabarty. Perhaps we can examine this concept of scale a bit more closely; *how do you stand on this, especially when it is used as a temporal concept?*

Laurent: You are raising here a deep and major question, which we shall have to return to more closely. In relation to scale, I wasn't thinking, at this stage of our discussion, about time scales *per se*, but the intensity of present material creations and disturbances of existing material memory, which is preserved within the ground. As Bruno Latour and Chris Witmore point out, these processes of transformation of our natural environment are, compared to the previous ones of our human history, simply beyond any normality – they are *cosmocolossal* writes Latour, *hypanthropical* says Witmore.[6] But let's put aside, for the moment, this question of a geo-archaeo/logical time, which is addressed in Chakrabarty's paper; I'll come back to it very soon. My first concern, as I said, is what this anthropocenic situation does to the practice of archaeology.

I believe it terminates archaeology, as we have known it. As you have pointed out, the flow of new data is so thick and rapid now that it has become impossible to integrate them into the usual archaeological discourse: they are far too numerous, continuously accumulating, making synthesis an impossible task. For the first time, as you said, theory-building can't keep up with the flood of data. So scholars retreat into more speculative work, far away from the noise and the trouble of the field: in the Anglo-American academic world, the archaeology of the contemporary past is a good example of such an archaeology which is generally not based on excavations and extensive data recording: an *above-ground* archaeology, as Latour would say, for which you just need to get a camera and a notebook.[7]

But the advent of the Anthropocene is also putting the conduct of archaeology in a deep crisis. It has become impossible to dig these 'anthropocenic' sites – such as airports, highways, infrastructures, suburbs... They are far too large, far too uniform, too repetitive. But above all, they are essentially made by machines, and I believe that archaeology has relatively little to say about machine-made creations, since archaeology is basically about the human: everything made, or experienced, by humans. And it is quite revealing, I guess, that, when surveys or excavations are carried out on sites of the contemporary past, it is always about human-scale features: a few rooms of a flat, a pit in the ground containing stuff, and always graves – as in any other period of traditional archaeology.

But I see your point, which is: let's be very careful about this concept of 'over-scale', since it tends to freeze any kind of thinking, when confronted by the enormity of this new anthropocenic situation; and so I do fully agree with you. On the other hand, I believe the damage done is so big that we can't fix it anymore with our good old conceptual tools: we can't bring the situation back to normal, or just rearrange it to keep it bearable.

What Chakrabarty points out in that paper is quite disturbing indeed: to put it bluntly, the times of 'natural' geology and 'anthropic' history are incompatible and so we lack any good historical framework to really encompass the nature of the Anthropocene. In other words, we don't know how to deal with a global history of the Earth, which would not necessarily be grasped from our own human perspective, especially when it is about us. In fact, the 'historicization' of the Anthropocene leads us into an aporia: either we try to integrate the Anthropocene into a human history of the planet looking for the realization of some sustainable future – but in this case we completely miss the specificity of the Anthropocene. Or we don't, looking instead for a long-term history of the 'Earth system' – but again we miss in this case the particularity of the Anthropocene. In fact, we are facing a hybrid monster: both natural and cultural – and the trouble is we don't know how to think chimeras.

The trick about the Anthropocene is that, in order to think the Anthropocene, we have to think *beyond* the Anthropocene: I mean from some place where we escape the Anthropocene. This place could be the future (after the cataclysm of the Anthropocene, somehow), but it could also be *beside* our post-industrial world. But whereabouts, you might ask? With indigenous cultures which are still here today, according to Baschet: after all, the advent of the Anthropocene is nothing other than the revelation of the lethal nature of Capitalism. Following this unsure path, Baschet aims to break from this *tyranny of the present* imposed on us by the spread of the Anthropocene. He looks for alternative models of time in Amerindian cultures, such as those of Chiapas, in Mexico.[8]

But I will send you back the same question: what do you think about this issue of the 'historicization' of the Anthropocene?

Gavin: Perhaps I am misunderstanding you but this question of the historicization of the Anthropocene to me is reminiscent of our earlier discussion about presentism as a historical phenomenon, as a period. And to think the Anthropocene then, like any period, is think outside it, which is I suppose what you also meant by thinking beyond it. Thinking outside any period, almost always means thinking after it – to be ahead of it, to project ourselves into a future when the Anthropocene is over. This reverses the normal order of things though; periodization is usually conducted with *hindsight*, but when defining the period of the present – whether that is the Anthropocene, Presentism or simply Modernity – requires *foresight* not hindsight. The trouble with foresight is how premature it always is – think of Postmodernism which proclaimed the end of Modernity from within yet turned out to really be just another version of Modernity. And I suppose the evidence of such failures is why Fukuyama proclaimed the end of history, there is nothing after Capitalism, we have reached the end of the road. Hartog elevated this into a wider regime of historicity, which Baschet contends we need to shatter, although I should say I have not read Baschet. At the same time, I cannot help thinking that we have got ourselves into this predicament by adopting a historicization of the present in the first place. How can you ever define an epoch or period within which you are living? Older generations of historians like Humboldt long warned of such follies, though we now ignore them.[9]

One way to look at this is to suggest there are two ways of understanding ourselves in time and history; one is historical, one that adopts periods and requires we adopt a position *outside* of history, after it, beyond it. Under this view, contemporary history is an oxymoron. It is impossible. The other is archaeological in the broad, philosophical sense of the term; it requires we adopt a position *inside* history, where there is no outside, and therefore no before or after. Time bends back on itself. For the present, this is essential – we cannot do otherwise simply because the *present never ends*. You can never catch up with it and go ahead of, except in some imaginary state. But we can stretch this never-ending present backwards quite a long time, though as with the end, origins are equally impossible to pin down. Modernity is archaeology not history because it reaches back to 1850, 1789 or 1550 depending on your perspective. The Anthropocene too is archaeology not history, though here we are dealing with much more temporal elasticity, where it starts as early as 12,000 years ago or as recently as 150 years ago.

So all this discussion of the historicization of the Anthropocene to me seem to conflate a historical with an archaeological understanding of what it is. I don't believe it is helpful to see the Anthropocene as historical, as a period, though we can of course. The same applies to Modernity. This is a different dilemma and conflation to that raised by Chakrabarty and also to how you framed it above. So if we think the Anthropocene as archaeological, not historical, then the point is precisely *not to think outside of it or beyond it* but rather to untangle it from within. Perhaps Baschet's suggestions for drawing on indigenous views of time are one way to achieve this, but I am not sure I would frame it in such historical terms as he seems to (or at least if I have understood your summary of him).

But what does this untangling involve? In part, it is about untangling the dichotomy of the natural and cultural; as you said, one of the features of the Anthropocene is that it is a hybrid, a mix of natural and cultural processes. But this is why I want us to discuss the problem of scale. Because we already know how to deal with hybrids; Latour through ANT and Viveiros de Castros through animism and indigenous ontologies among many others have already taught us ways to address this forced dichotomy of culture and nature. If the dichotomy re-emerges with the Anthropocene, it is because it is the different time scales involved that have forced them apart again. It is scale we need to look at here and more particularly how it distracts us from what really matters: the time of things, whether these are cultural or natural.

I hope this answers your question of historization and the Anthropocene – and if you still want to postpone the discussion of scale, I am happy to. *But do you agree that the historicization of the Anthropocene is a red herring or if not, perhaps you can explain further why you think it is a problem?*

Laurent: You are coming at this from another angle than me and to the point I have tried to make about what happens with any attempt to historicize the present, no matter if it is Hartog's Presentism or Chakrabarty's Anthropocene: it reveals the dichotomy between historicity and temporality, stressing – as Agamben does for instance – that our only relevant access to this matter is through temporality. And temporality, seen as the condition under which we experience not only the present, but also time, is *par excellence* the field of archaeology. It is in this sense that archaeology could be a tool to overcome the deep crisis created by the spread of the Anthropocene.

And this archaeological tool is not only methodological or theoretical; it is also strongly political, since, as I have tried to stress, archaeology is basically attached to the human – and it is precisely the human which is attacked and threatened by what the Anthropocene produces: the over-exploitation of fossil resources, the financialization of the human economy, the destruction of the human landscape – I mean the *ecoumene*, the landscape which is inhabitable by the humans.[10] Fighting against the Anthropocene is fighting against this economic and political global model personified by Reagan's to Trump's governments. It is fighting along with the indigenous people, and the inheritance of pre-industrial cultures, to defend the Earth's resources against their degradation and extinction. It is preserving and transmitting the material memory of the *ecoumene*.

So yes, if you take temporality seriously enough – as the specific internal time of things and beings – it makes traditional historical time explode. This is what Walter Benjamin meant, in his own manner of expression, when he claimed that historicism was a form of *barbary*: the barbary of the contemporary industrial world. And this question is not only a problem of contemporary times or Modernity, if you prefer, but indeed of all times in our human history. As archaeologists, we are standing on this side of temporality and not of historicity – which is an artificial concept, fabricated by our cultural tradition. Archaeological time – the time of objects and material remains – clearly demonstrates that historical time is nothing else than a dangerous illusion.

For sure, if we keep thinking that the archaeological task is about historicizing the past, we are actually in big trouble. But the spread of the Anthropocene also brings us some good news. This *never ending present*, which is its specific temporality, gives us access to still incompletely explored areas of knowledge about the relationship between past, present and future. It reveals the central place occupied by memory or transformission. In this sense, we may use the temporality of the Anthropocene as a weapon to overcome the pressure imposed on us by the Anthropocene.

I don't know if we understand each other well enough yet so could you explain how you would answer this question yourself?

Gavin: I fear we don't understand each other right now. To what question are you referring? If it is the one I asked you, then there is no question to answer in my mind. The historicization of the Anthropocene is not a problem, because I don't think it makes sense to see the Anthropocene as a historical period like the Holocene or the Neolithic. The temporality of the Anthropocene is another matter however and again, for me this is a problem because it entangles time with the metrological concept of scale. From what I can gather, we both seem to stress the temporality over the historicity of the Anthropocene as the important thing; but where I want to talk about scale, you want to talk about the present. If so, the question becomes – how do we bridge these two concepts so we can start talking together again? Because I fear – and you also sensed it too Laurent – we now seem to be talking past each other. So I guess we need to slow down again. How do we build a bridge – or have I even identified the right places ('the present' and 'scale') on each side of this divide where we should build a bridge?

Laurent: I don't believe there is any divide between us; but, to take an image, we are travelling on different planets, following our own orbit; being sometimes very close, sometimes quite far away... So yes, we both agree about the crucial importance of temporality versus the historicization of the Anthropocene. However, I don't think the metrological concept of time is a problem in itself, if you take it for what it is: just a means of measurement. And I would add this metrological measurement of time is valuable for revealing the 'true time' of temporality – when it makes for instance my miner's lamps 'snakes around' the straight line of metrological time. It is a necessary dialectical relationship.

The trouble, as Chakrabarty stresses, is what we put on this metrological time, considering it is the 'real time' of history, cultures and civilizations. This is deeply paradoxical, since the existence of periods, ages and eras is obvious – as we are particularly aware, as archaeologists – but the trick is that this has nothing to do with any historical meaning. You are working in Iceland, where the human occupation of the island dates back only to the early Middle Ages: does this mean that there was 'nothing' before that? You have also been working overseas: if Australian aboriginal material culture lacks any clear trend of transformation over tens of thousands of years, does it mean that it is deprived of any 'history'? So, what does this mean, precisely, the *historicizing* of any period of time? Isn't it projecting our own understanding of Western history – moving from prehistoric 'primitivity' to historic civilization – onto a world that never worked like that?

Yes, you are right, I am fascinated by the present, seen here as the place of the burst of the future – its transformation into an 'historic period', I would say. Let me tell you a little story. A very good friend of mine called Jérôme Prieur is a writer and a film-maker. For the last 15 years, he has been making a series of documentaries about Nazi Germany and WW2 using all kinds of images that were produced during those times – propaganda films as well as amateurs ones. Within this huge mass of pictures, he has found no recording of the historical events of this period. The Wannsee conference was not filmed, for instance; and, in most cases, some other images have been used to illustrate the dramatic events of that time: German troops marching along the Champs Elysées in Paris to illustrate the invasion of France, for instance. Most of the images shot during these years display something else: the daily life, everywhere. Of course, the shooting of these pictures is the result of a choice but regardless, they have recorded the temporality of WW2 – and this is what is deeply fascinating about these scattered pieces of films.

What is the problem with scale, you ask? Seen from within, in a truly archaeological way, any period of time is lacking historical time.

History has never existed, as it has been reconstructed. The Anthropocene is digging out this paradox: history is both real – it has really happened once; it is really happening now – and history is simultaneously only a perception, a 'way of seeing' the past. The only real time is that of temporality, of the present, of archaeology, of things and beings. Physicists actually say: time is not describable in terms of entities but interactions. We should think about that.

But tell me what do you mean with scale in this discussion? It is maybe my fault since I perhaps don't see clearly what you mean by that ...

Gavin: What I mean by scale is perhaps a little different to how you have framed it but not much. Yes, it is a metrology, a tool for measuring time. But as I see it, a temporal metrology has two facets. One is simply measuring duration, using a regular unit such as years. This is what we mean by chronology, which I think is what you were referring too. But the other facet involves inter-changing the unit of measure (e.g. years for centuries), that is, a tool for zooming in or out, taking larger or shorter spans of time as a focus. This more specific aspect is what I mean by scale. Archaeologists and historians have usually evoked it to signify the importance of historical distance – that the more you zoom out, the larger and longer-term processes come into focus. Come too close and you see nothing. Humboldt's analogy of viewing a painting is a classic example; come too close and it's all a swirl of colours. You need to stand back to see what the picture is. Now since Braudel (if not before), we have qualified this to say that what you see, depends on your scale of analysis. Zooming out certainly makes things visible that before were invisible, but the converse is equally true. Zoom out too far and you miss little details. For an art historian studying technique, coming up close to observe swirls of colour reveals other things besides what the painting depicts – brush strokes, blending, layering etc. Now this is all very good until you suddenly want to talk about how two (or more) scales relate. If we leave the analogy of Humboldt's painting behind and come back to Chakrabarty, the problem is, one scale reveals one thing – climate change, global warming etc., another scale reveals human decisions, policy actions, consumer choice. How to bridge two vastly different scales? Ever since Braudel, we have been grappling with this problem, unsuccessfully, I think.

The reason I wanted to talk about scale is to underline that the problem here is part of our own making. We have mistaken an historical operation – scaling, zooming in and out – for an historical process. Listen to how archaeologists talk about this; they talk about different processes operating at different scales, things unfolding over longer or shorter durations, etc. What *was* an historiographical operation – zooming in and out – has subtly transformed into an historical ontology about the world. What if we stop and ask ourselves: how might we understand history without the concept of scale? This, I suppose, is what I wanted to suggest as a (possible) response to Chakrabarty's dilemma.

But now I find that in posing this question, I come right up against your point: history has never existed, it is always a retrospective operation, a reconstruction. If that is the case, then history has no ontology separate from the historiographic operation, and so scale is surely unavoidable. Perhaps, but then again, maybe what I mean by an historical ontology is the same as what you mean by temporality or the present. I do think we are probably talking about the same thing here. A non-scalar history is one which always takes place in the present; a non-scalar history is, in fact, an archaeology. It is seeing history not as a serial temporality, each moment or present replacing the next but as a stretched out or elastic temporality, an extended present. Elastic time is not the same as scalar time; stretching (or shearing) and scaling are two very different topological operations, as any geometry student can tell you.

Now although the Anthropocene is perhaps testing our abilities to stretch this present to an extent previously unimagined, essentially I don't think there is otherwise anything intrinsically unique about this 'epoch' in relation to archaeology or our understanding of time. Possibly you and I personally ascribe it a different weight in our 'philosophies of time', and that may also have detracted me from seeing the deeper commonalities of our positions. So rather let me focus on these commonalities.

This notion of the extended present is of course something I have borrowed from physicists, where it has a rather different meaning. But you also drew a connection to physicists where 'time is not describable in terms of entities, but interactions. We should think about that'. Yes we should, because this is what history as an extended present is ultimately about; the way interactions between things creates, shapes or nullifies time. *But how would you think about this?*

Laurent: What you said about scales is amazing, since this is exactly the problem we have been facing in the course of our *Briquetage de la Seille* project. It was not only a question of times scales, but simultaneously of spatial ones; I mean it was not only about encompassing different processes occurring along various durations, as you mentioned, since these processes were also displaying different features along various spatial units within the valley. For instance, the same phenomenon – the artificial filling of the river channels around the Iron Age saltworks, for example – had quite different results, depending on whether we were observing the immediate surroundings of the workshops, or larger areas of the floodplain downstream. So, we soon realized that we were confronted by an entanglement of many spatial and temporal scales; the key question becoming how these processes were '*infusing*' and '*percolating*' from one scale to another – simultaneously at different scales, in fact. Historical time was dissolving into a multiplicity of interactions, just as you said. So I would say, to paraphrase your last definition of archaeology, that it is not really non-scalar, when, on the contrary, history is basically scalar: archaeology is rather *multi-scalar*; this multiplicity of interactions occurring at a diversity of scales 'nullifying' indeed historical time.

So, in this sense, archaeology is fundamentally 'anti-historicist', to reframe Benjamin's thought, since it is based on temporality – again the multi-scalar time of things and beings. *Are we on the same page, now?*

Gavin: Yes and no. Yes, there is a multiplicity to archaeological time which is at odds with the singularity of chronology or metrological time. And for sure, it is anti-historicist in the sense that most history tends to adopt a singular time (though again, we should not forget Braudel who argued for multiple time scales – even if, in the end, he seemed to privilege the *longue durée*). And yet no. For I have a deep problem with this notion of multi-scalar time because it conflates an analytical tool for an ontology. *Time is not multi-scalar – our metrology is.* Now at one level, using the term multi-scalar to refer to this multiplicity of time is understandable – it does capture something of the fact that different processes, events or causalities seem to operate over longer or shorter spans of chronological time, as in your example of the briquetage sites. But the problem with using the concept of scale to capture this multiplicity is that it mixes together *at least two different kinds of multiplicity*: duration and speed. We say something is long-term if it lasts a long time, but we also say it's long-term if it changes really slowly. But they are not the same thing. Using one term to cover two very different temporal phenomena lands us in all kinds of problems, not least the problem of how to integrate or talk about the interaction of things which have different temporalities.

Summing this up best I can, scale is a property of our metrology which allows us to articulate the multiplicity of time, but we must not confuse it for that multiplicity. To understand the multiplicity if time, we need to pay much closer attention to the nature of change, to its forms, its different manifestations which are deeply connected to different materialities. My feeling is adopting the concept of scale to address multiplicity has distracted us from this more important issue of the multiplicity of change. But I am not sure if many archaeologists would agree with me on this; scale and the concept of multi-scalar time is such an entrenched and normal part of our disciplinary vocabulary now, it is hard to see past it. But I would argue that we need to build a new vocabulary nonetheless.

But perhaps you can tell me more about how you see temporal multiplicity operating in your Briquetage de la Seille project; do you think, given what I have said, there is a way to talk about this multiplicity without invoking scale?

Laurent: Again, I believe we address these questions from two opposite ends: yours is rather theoretical and philosophical – and is perhaps a bit too rigid, I guess – whereas mine comes directly from my field experience and is certainly lacking any solid theoretical framework.

In the Seille valley, we begun looking at the salt production techniques of the Iron Age, but we quickly realized it was unproductive: we had to look at the archaeology of the valley, from the beginning of the Holocene to the contemporary period, and to study not only these prehistoric workshops but also their immediate environment and beyond the area of the valley at large.

The Seille valley project was truly an open-air methodological lab. We had a team digging archaeological test-trenches and open excavations of course, but also people studying micromorphology, some others bio-stratigraphy and geo-archaeology through systematic coring. More broadly, we also had a team of geophysicists surveying the valley, looking for all kinds of features, both natural and anthropic. A first challenge was to correlate all these observations both in time and space, since we were addressing different processes occurring at different places, different durations and different speeds. Archaeological dating was not enough, since the data were mostly coming from various sediment deposits; so we chose to prioritize OMS and C14 dating, wherever this was possible. This provided us with a metrologic chronological framework, which was, however, essentially probabilistic. And of course, it was a problem to reconstruct an accurate 'history', since this was impossible with such a fuzzy probabilistic chronology, to precisely identify chains of causes and effects. We just had the material result of changes, always already transformed by its post-history.

So we recognized that, as you have stressed, we had to focus not on this absent history but on these present material products of change. And here, again, metrologic time was very useful to reveal both duration and speed, since the nature of the material remains had a strong impact on the behaviour of these changes and their manifestation. To give you just a few examples, the tossing of industrial waste around the workshops immediately created a significant 'chronological dilation' locally through a rapid accumulation of deposits. But, further on, it was releasing a long-term dynamic, whose effect was delayed: the alluvial filling of the valley did not really begin until a few centuries later and was dramatically accelerating towards the end of the Middle Ages, obviously fed by external processes – such as wood clearing, as was obvious from the pollen records. On the other hand, in response to the gradual filling of the valley, the Seille river was cutting channels and meanders across this accumulating mass of alluvial deposits, while on the slopes around it, erosion was badly cutting any prior archaeological formations.

In a word, it was complicated. But it became clear that our good old historical tools were ineffective to encompass what we were dealing with: it was impossible to describe this complexity within some linear history. We were only faced with a diversity of interactive changes, displaying transforming effects over time. It was obvious too that the 'historical lens' – I mean seeing the past as a sequence of events, each one taking the place of the previous one – was particularly wrong: the material stuff that had been created, or transformed before was still there in subsequent periods of time, still constraining or shaping future trajectories.

In other words, at each moment, the past was still present, as a persistent and active material presence. To put it clearly, we had to turn the traditional archaeological approach upside down: I mean we had to stop trying to use archaeological data to feed a reconstruction of an artificial history, but rather exploit the metrologic tools at our disposal to try to encompass these archaeological processes of change and transformission *in themselves*. So, I agree with you that we have to implement another vocabulary, but, more deeply, we have to develop another way of thinking these archaeological dynamics.

But how? I believe by looking at other disciplines in the Human Sciences which are dealing with the same kind of problematic. Psychoanalysis, for instance, which primarily deals with memory – that is to say with the persistence of the past, which has never passed. It deals with a different time, which is not a historical one: again, this is the time of temporality, in other words the time of the past within the present: archaeological time *par excellence*.

Gavin: Well there it is; you say I am coming at this from a more philosophical and too rigid angle while you are dealing with more concrete, empirical problems. But my point is not abstract or rigid at all; it is simply that we all use abstract, philosophical concepts all the time to come to terms with our archaeology and so we just need to be vigilant about those terms, especially the ones that seem so straightforward like scale. Maybe this is the influence of Anglophone analytical philosophy and especially the Oxford school of Ordinary Language philosophy which saw most philosophical problems as illusions created by the words we used (in my twenties, I was deeply into Wittgenstein). If I seemed too abstract, it was simply a provocation to go back to our concrete problems and re-think them without using one word. So what happens when you describe the Iron Age salt production project without using the word 'scale'? You talk about dilation, delay, acceleration, persistence – terms which capture the subtleties of your material. We don't need to align them under a single concept like multi-scalar; I would argue *that* is what is rigid here. Rather let's just stick with these terms and explore what they mean and how they intersect. This is ultimately my goal here, and I think, yours too.

If there is any difference, it lies in the sources we use to draw inspiration from to reflect on our language and our problems; for you, psycho-analysis is obviously a major source and I can see it has been extremely productive for you. For me, it is probably more philosophy. But such difference is only good. I think one of the reasons we can have such a fruitful discussion as this is because we share different sources of inspiration – we get to see something of each other's personal journey and perspective on what are mostly shared matters of concern. As a result, we see our own positions in a different light; we learn from each other.

Notes

1. R. Harrison, C. DeSilvey, C. Holtorf, S. Macdonald, N. Bartolini, E. Breithoff, H. Fredheim, A. Lyons, S. May, J. Morgan, and S. Penrose. *Heritage Futures. Comparative Approaches to Natural and Cultural Heritage Practices* (London: UCL Press, 2020).
2. T. Piketty, *Capital in the Twenty-First Century* (Harvard: Harvard University Press, 2014).
3. Jacques Le Goff, *Faut-il vraiment découper l'histoire en tranches?* (Paris: Le Seuil, 2014): J. Le Goff, *Must we divide history into periods?* (New York: Columbia University Press, 2015).
4. D. Chakrabarty 2018. Anthropocene Time. *History and Theory* 57, no.1 (2018): 5–32.
5. See, for example, the important volume by J. Robb & T. Pauketat (eds.), *Big Histories, Human Lives: Tackling Problems of Scale in Archaeology* (Santa Fe: School of Advanced Research, 2013).
6. B. Latour, *Face à Gaïa. Huit conférences sur le nouveau régime climatique* (Paris: La Découverte 2015), 9-10; B. Latour, 2017. *Facing Gaia. Eight Lectures on the New Climate Regime*, (Cambridge: Polity Press, 2017); Christopher Witmore, 'Archaeology, the Anthropocene and the Hypanthropocene', *Journal of Contemporary Archaeology*, 1, no.1 (2014): 128–132.
7. B. Latour, *Où atterrir? Comment s'orienter en politique* (Paris: La Découverte, 2017); B. Latour, *Down to Earth: Politics in the New Climate Regime* (Cambridge: Polity Press, 2018)
8. J. Baschet, *Défaire la tyrannie du présent. Temporalités émergentes et futurs inédits* (Paris: La Découverte, 2018).
9. W. von Humboldt, 'On the Historian's Task'. *History and Theory* 6, no.1 (1967): 57–71.
10. A. Berque, *Écoumène. Introduction à l'étude des milieux humains* (Paris: Belin, 2000); and by the same author, *Milieu et identité humaine. Pour un dépassement de la modernité* (Paris: Donner lieu, 2010).

Bibliography

Baschet, J. *Défaire la tyrannie du présent. Temporalités émergentes et futurs inédits.* Paris: La Découverte, 2018.

Berque, A. *Écoumène. Introduction à l'étude des milieux humains.* Paris: Belin, 2000.

Berque, A. *Milieu et identité humaine. Pour un dépassement de la modernité.* Paris: Donner lieu, 2010.

Chakrabarty, D. 'Anthropocene Time'. *History and Theory* 57, no.1 (2018): 5–32.

Harrison, R., C. DeSilvey, C. Holtorf, S. Macdonald, N. Bartolini, E. Breithoff, H. Fredheim, A. Lyons, S. May, J. Morgan, and S. Penrose. *Heritage Futures. Comparative Approaches to Natural and Cultural Heritage Practices.* London: UCL Press, 2020.

Humboldt, W. von, 'On the Historian's Task'. *History and Theory* 6, no.1 (1967): 57–71.

Latour, B. *Face à Gaïa. Huit conférences sur le nouveau régime climatique.* Paris: La Découverte, 2015.

Latour, B. *Facing Gaia. Eight Lectures on the New Climate Regime,* Cambridge: Polity Press, 2017.

Latour, B. *Où atterrir? Comment s'orienter en politique.* Paris: La Découverte, 2017.

Latour, B. *Down to Earth: Politics in the New Climate Regime.* Cambridge: Polity Press, 2018.

Le Goff, J. *Faut-il vraiment découper l'histoire en tranches?* Paris: Le Seuil, 2014.

Le Goff, J. *Must We Divide History into Periods?* New York: Columbia University Press, 2015.

Piketty, T. *Capital in the Twenty-First Century.* Harvard: Harvard University Press, 2014.

Robb, J. and T. Pauketat (eds.). *Big Histories, Human Lives: Tackling Problems of Scale in Archaeology,* Santa Fe: School of Advanced Research, 2013.

Witmore, C. 'Archaeology, the Anthropocene and the Hypanthropocene', *Journal of Contemporary Archaeology,* 1, no.1 (2014): 128–132.

6 Time out

In this last chapter, we pause and look back over all we have said – not to sum up but rather to reflect on what was not said. What did we omit from our discussion that our readers might have expected or liked to hear more about? Why did we omit them: did we forget, did we deliberately avoid them, or were we just too blinkered to notice matters that are of major concern to our colleagues?

Laurent: Surely, Gavin, a lot of people are not going to be very happy about what we have said here. Some are going to say that our perception of archaeology is outdated because we don't acknowledge the latest developments in archaeological dating, ignore recent approaches like deep history or underestimate the role of time in other fields within the Human Sciences. How would you answer such critiques?

Gavin: You are right Laurent, there is a lot we don't discuss. This after all, was a dialogue exploring the intersections of our interests and inevitably things will get left out, things which lie outside both our interests. And yes, we are both getting old and no longer the young scholars who met in Cambridge more than quarter of a century ago! But I think there are good reasons why we ignore some of these things you mention.

Let's take the issues of recent developments in absolute dating, specifically Bayesian modelling of C14 dates on the one hand and deep history on the other.[1] In some ways, the two are diametrically opposed: where deep history revels in the long term, the new Bayesian methods are all about bringing the resolution down to human generational scales. If deep history is about making history more like archaeology in its long-term view, Bayesian dating is all about making archaeology more like history with its tracing of events at the human scale. But of course both, in the end, share the same view of time and the past as a sequential, linear flow. In this sense, while I think these Bayesian methods are marvellous and will enable us to produce far more sophisticated narratives, they don't really change anything when it comes to our understanding of time. These developments are being described as revolutionary and in some ways, they are; but it all depends on what kind of revolution you are talking about. This is a revolution in

DOI: 10.4324/9781003183600-6

chronology – it increases our scale of resolution which does have all kinds of important consequences. But at the end of the day, nothing has changed about our concept of time, which is still founded on chronology in these cases. Both deep history and Bayesian dating are just part of the same phenomenon: expanding the scale of chronology upward and downward respectively. Neither dislodges chronology from its hegemonic position within archaeology, in fact they just reinforce it. So in terms of the discussion we have been having throughout these conversations, both seem exceptionally conventional.

Regarding other issues like the discussion of time in other disciplines and its relation to archaeology – well of course we have engaged with this, albeit selectively; philosophy, history, psycho-analysis, art history and physics have all cropped up. I suppose the one major absence has been ethnography and anthropology, especially the exploration of indigenous concepts of time (though you briefly alluded to this in your discussion of Baschet). I think this is a fairer critique.

How do you feel about this though? Since you brought it up …

Laurent: I believe you made the right point: something new is not the same as a novelty. A true novelty changes your way of seeing and thinking. There haven't been that many actual novelties in our field in the last fifty years; in this sense, processualism and postprocessualism were real novelties - they created a paradigm change, as Thomas Kuhn would have said[2]. But expanding the scale of chronology in both directions – towards 'deep time' on one hand and 'micro-events' on the other – doesn't mean changing the way chronology remains considered: basically as the expression of historical change. That is to say, as the very frame of history.

Nevertheless I wouldn't be so critical as you are: such extensions of chronology push the study of the human past – let's call it the historical disciplines at large – to its very limits. A similar process has occurred over the last 50 years in the discipline of history, with Braudel's *longue durée* and Ginzburg's micro-history for instance.[3] Both address the question of the place of the *Anthropos* within these macro- and micro-durations. Indeed over the very long term, it becomes clear that cultures, societies, or economic systems don't primarily drive the historical transformations of landscapes and environments: it is much more about natural processes, or more precisely a mix of anthropic and ecological interactions. This disintegration of the *Anthropos* is even more obvious when one is dealing with the pre-human past – I mean pre-*sapiens* prehistory.

On the other hand, at the microscopic scale of actions and behavior of individuals, the same sort of question occurs. In his famous *Cheese and the Worms*, the Italian historian Carlo Ginzburg tells us the story of Menocchio's trial, a miller of the 16th Century, who was accused of being a heretic and ultimately condemned to be burnt alive.[4] Belonging to the peasant class, Menocchio knew how to read, write and count. He wasn't educated, but he was smart and aspired to think for himself. Since the minutes of his trial have been miraculously preserved, we can listen to Mennochio's answers to the judges, which are very often much more sensible than the speeches of the magistrates... But then you wonder: in what way is Menocchio a man of his time? Or, to put it another way: how does this micro-history relate to the global history of 16th Century Italy, for instance? Isn't it rather something else – a field closer to ethnography than history in itself?

We may ask ourselves the same kind of questions when we are recording such micro-events within archaeological sites. Of course, in some cases, it is possible to get a very accurate dating of these 'archaeological instants', but the question remains: how does it relate to a more global history of the place or its time, or does it at all? At the other end of the chronological scale, we were facing a similar problem, when dealing with the long environmental history of, for example, the Seille valley, which runs from the beginning of the Holocene. In this case, we soon realized that, in fact, we weren't doing anything related to a 'deep past' in itself – since it lacked any direct archaeological evidence. We just used it as a framework, or a background if you prefer, of the archaeological phenomenon we were specially observing: the spread of briquetage salt production of the Iron Age and its impact on the later environment and settlements.

So, in a way, these extreme extensions of the chronological scale do challenge the meaning of our archaeological quest: what are we looking for, what sense are we making from what we find in the ground? *Surely many of our readers will wonder: fair enough, but how can archaeological time, as they approach it, enlighten other perceptions of time in related fields of the Human Sciences; how do they articulate this with an understanding of the* Anthropos, *the human phenomenon?*

Gavin: Ok, I see what you are saying now and concede that I may have been too hasty in my dismissal of these developments, although as you already point out, these extensions of our chronology, pulling in two different directions – this tendency has been around before Bayesian modelling and deep history came on the scene. It was there in Annales history and Braudel as you pointed out and archaeologists taking up Annales approaches in the late 1980s and 1990s rehearsed these same tensions, which were carried over into subsequent concerns with scale, as we touched on in our earlier conversations.[5] But the issue you raise is not about scale – just as it wasn't earlier perhaps, even if I wanted to drive it in that direction. The issue is about the *Anthropos*, as you say. So let's be blunt here: what we are addressing I suppose is human time. What is this? Is it even a real or coherent phenomenon? Or is it a creation of the Enlightenment, like Foucault's subject 'Man' or humanity?[6] Is there a shared temporality for history, archaeology, psychology or ethnography? Is there a shared subject, humanity? In the wake of posthumanism, we know this is a complex issue that has many dimensions and in relation to time, the answer would seem equally complex. It isn't just that there is one human time but many, but rather that these many temporalities cannot be separated from the temporalities of other species, other things and ultimately, our planet as the Anthropocene debate reminds us.

In this sense, deep history is potentially more of a radical shift than Bayesian modelling; the latter after all seems to re-affirm a rather traditional humanism and singular view of human temporality, though of course it needn't. Deep history however, conceptually at least, seems to take on more explicitly this posthumanist re-framing, insofar as it acknowledges the problematic boundary between Nature and Culture. But together, perhaps both throw up a sharper problem than neither do on their own. That human time is both something that happens over more than two million years AND over a decade. What does that do to our sense of being human?

I am reminded here of the classic character in contemporary fiction, the immortal. I think of Christopher Lambert playing *Highlander* in the movie of the same name from the 1980s, or Brad Pitt playing Louis de Point du Lac in *Interview with a Vampire* from the 1990s. These characters are weighed down by the burden of immortality, living for centuries. Humans ultimately cannot cope with immortality, life needs to be finite. And of course, these characters aren't really human. But what has this got to do with archaeology? Well isn't it exactly the same problem? How would an immortal write history? We all know what human time is like because we live it; and maybe most disciplines like history and ethnography and even psychology can work within this sense of human time, because their sources speak it and live it too. But with archaeology, we are faced with something else; we faced with sources which aren't quite human. I am not suggesting this is a problem unique to archaeology or that other disciplines cannot deal with a 'posthuman temporality'; clearly they can and so. But I do think for archaeologists, it's harder to ignore.

I am not sure any of this really answers your question, but it does perhaps hint that archaeologists might be in a position to address the question of the Anthropos from a very different perspective to other disciplines in the humanities and social sciences, especially when it deals with time. I guess you would take a similar view, or what?

Laurent: Yes I do, although I am not so enthusiastic about Christophe Lambert's performance as an actor!... As archaeologists, we are the only ones, indeed, to see the effect of time on artefacts, places and landscapes – how they are transformed through a multiplicity of different durations. Even historians don't see this as directly as we do: they work on scattered documents and they reconstruct time at quite a local scale. We don't: we just watch it, on our archaeological sites, along durations far beyond, as you said, the scale of the human lifespan. As you pointed out, this is not just a question of scale, it is also basically a question of interpreting the *Anthropos. So people who aren't familiar with archaeology would certainly ask: but how different is it, compared to history, anthropology or sociology and psychology?*

Gavin: Now you are making me do the hard work! How is time in archaeology different? To some extent, it isn't of course. With all these disciplines, we share a concern for dates and chronology; for social and collective memory; for biography and the life cycle of things and households; for culturally variable systems of time reckoning, routines and rituals. These are all classically within the realm of 'human time' and in pursuing them, we are re-affirming what connects us to these other disciplines. They are also themes that have tended to dominate much of the discussion on time in archaeology. As topics, they clearly have some temporal elasticity – they address not only the short term of lived human experience but also traverse centuries of social and cultural history. Perhaps that is why they are so dominant – they seem to successfully bridge the short and long-term. But only if the long-term is not *too* long. Such as when the long-term expands to cover millennia. Only archaeology has to deal with such long time spans, although this is also the rationale behind deep history, to urge historians to also consider this. But when you do engage with such spans of time, all these traditional topics start to look irrelevant. How does collective memory or generational succession work over millennia?

I just read a fascinating paper about the possible (likely even) theory that Stonehenge was originally in Wales but was dismantled and moved (partially or wholly) to the Salisbury Plain at the end of the 4th millennium BCE by Welsh migrants.[7] The evidence is quite stunning, but what is even more remarkable is that the paper suggests some vestige of this event was preserved in collective memory and occurs, distorted and mangled in a 12th Century CE account. This account is largely taken to be fictional today and of little historic value. Yet there it is. I suppose one might claim this is what happens to collective memory after 4000 years; it becomes so twisted, re-cycled and re-contextualized that even if it does survive, it's barely recognizable. And yet, look at the archaeological remains; yes, they too have been mangled and twisted, but somehow their message is far more readable. Traces of the dismantling of Stonehenge – bang, right in your face, not garbled through the mouth of an interpreter who doesn't give you much cause for credibility anyway.

So what am I saying here? That archaeological remains are more objective or truthful? No. That archaeological or material remains articulate a temporality that exceeds, or is indeed quite different, from the temporality of human traditions? Not quite, because these remains are *part of* human traditions, as much as oral and written storytelling. Rather it is simply that human time looks different when you consider these archaeological and material things *alongside* the others. But what is this difference? From what I have said, you might think this is solely about the longevity of materials, of the archaeological; that the material traces of Stonehenge are more durable than its stories. This certainly fits with the usual explanation for what makes archaeology different:

its access to the long-term. This is an old and over-repeated mantra –
and of course it is true; archaeological sources seem to cover a much
broader time-span than written records, though one should be
careful in under-valuing the potential of traditional myths and oral
history for spanning millennia, as we just saw in the case of
Stonehenge. But I think there is more to this issue of longevity or
durability than simply brute persistence. What this 'more' is, I am not
sure I can articulate very well, though we have touched on it in our
earlier conversations.

*Perhaps now is the right moment for you to take over ... what do you
think is different about archaeological time?*

Laurent: It is a time of things; that is to say, some sort of 'extra-
human' time, as you put it. I mean that archaeological time,
although being based on artefacts made by humans, is not
completely human, or more precisely not entirely *conscious*. I
have always been fascinated by typo-chronology (yes, I
know; it's a bit weird!). When you look at morphological
transformations over several centuries, of the cutting edges
of some Bronze Age axes, for instance, and you see them
becoming larger and larger over time, you may wonder: what
really drives this process? Is it only human intentionality, or
could it be the case that the transformation of these artefacts
enjoys, somehow, its own dynamic? Isn't it in fact a
combination of these two different forces?

Survival is indeed one of the most fascinating phenomena we can
observe in archaeology. I also read about this amazing story with
Stonehenge. It is unsettling news, since it is about the transmission
of a very ancient inheritance which is reincorporated into a
different present, although nearly 5000 years old. This is the
kind of information that is provided *par excellence* by archaeology. One of my other interests is Early Celtic Art, and the way
time and space are expressed in these creations of the European
Iron Age. By that, I mean that I look at the structure of visual
space in which shapes are projected and the succession of temporal
sequences through which they are built; I don't care about the
usual questions of style, symbolism and so on – I just focus on
planes of visual projection and succession of layouts.[8] And like
Stonehenge, you see that, if shapes may change over time and
appear in distant places, their inner structure tends to remain.

I have been working for instance at the *Pilier des Nautes*, a stone pillar found scattered in several pieces beneath Notre-Dame's choir in 1711.[9] It depicts a combination of Celtic and Roman gods, organized on different levels, translating under Tiberius' reign the structure of the Celtic pantheon by incorporating Roman equivalents. These gods are projected onto a spatial distribution, ordering the hierarchy of the different 'worlds' they belong to and their place in the annual cycle according to their orientation towards cardinal directions. Here you see a specifically Celtic structure surviving in the early Roman period, under some sort of Roman disguise. The monument and the gods look Roman, but they remain Celtic. You even find that this Celtic 'iconological structure' has been integrated into much more distant creations, both in time and space: for instance, in the early Christian stones crosses of the Irish Early Middle Ages, more than a thousand years later ... There are indeed the very same schemes of spatial distribution in the figures, which are now applied to the depiction of Old and the New Testament characters and events.

So as you said, archaeological time is not just about a broader time-span than other sources of the human past: it reveals unsuspected processes, which otherwise literally jump over time and space. They obviously take place beyond our little bubble of 'conscious time' – this more or less immediate time of history, ethnography or sociology. I would rather call this vast and unexplored field, by contrast, 'unconscious time' – the time specifically revealed by archaeology. It is unconscious, indeed, since it is clear, for instance, that the Irish priests had absolutely no idea of Gaulish pre-Roman culture; but they nevertheless reproduced some of its distinctive features. Therefore, this archaeological time is obscure and hard to figure out, within our conventional categories of thinking. But we try to do it.

Thinking back to what you said at the beginning of this chapter, I believe we have to ask for some indulgence from our readers. There is a lot of things we haven't talked about, both because we didn't have them in mind and also because we are less familiar with some of these fields of knowledge or works – at least in my case. But I would add that, thanks to this dialogue, we have both (re)discovered, through the other's eye, aspects we had previously neglected or underestimated. So this book truly has to be taken as a 'work in progress'. *Are there issues, within what you talked about, you would like to make clearer for our readers before we finish this conversation?*

Gavin: I don't know Laurent – to be honest, I am sure there are lots of issues that I could clarify, but then this will probably depend on the reader. We are no doubt both aware that this conversation might sometimes have become too introverted, as if it were a private conversation to which a reader, especially one not familiar with our work, may feel excluded. This is a risk that comes with the territory. And yet some of these issues may lack clarity even to us. We have discussed a lot of concepts here and we are not only trying to understand each other, we also trying to understand these concepts. So I have no doubt we did not do proper justice to issues such as entropy, emergence, survival or persistence, and if the reader finds our discussion sometimes unclear, I think in part this will be due to the fact we are still struggling with these ideas too – or at least I am!

Another risk of our discussion is that because of the conversational format, one inevitably relaxes certain rules of etiquette or even scholarly expression so that one may not always express something in the most appropriate manner. It is easy to stereotype or generalize in such a situation, and probably we are both guilty of this. For example, I am sure my treatment of time perspectivism was too abbreviated and doesn't reflect the diversity and complexity of work out there, especially as I engage with this in my other writings in a more respectful way (I hope!).

Another stereotype is perhaps the difference between Continental and Anglo-American styles of thinking which dogged our whole correspondence; do we give it too much weight? Perhaps you should answer this, especially as I feel this may be something you feel more strongly about.

Laurent: Oh yes, I do sincerely apologize if anyone could feel offended by anything I have said – as this wasn't at all the point of our discussion. We spoke freely – like the old friends we are. But we think and feel differently and this isn't just a question of personality. When living abroad for quite a long time, you discover how you are also the product of your own culture. I realized I was French at Cambridge, although I thought earlier I had no special cultural or 'national' identity. And by the way, this was precisely the reason why I wanted to connect with Anglo-American research. This doesn't mean I am proud of my identity – not at all! – but I know in which way I am different.

You don't feel the same as an insider of the Anglo-American tradition, because it is also a matter of cultural hegemony. There have been times, around the end the 19th Century and the beginning of the 20th, when everything French was desirable, distinctive and prestigious. It was classy to wear French clothes, to speak French – in a word to affect being French. In such a situation, you don't realize, from the inside, that what seems to be universal to you is in fact basically provincial. You just wonder why everyone on earth isn't French or doesn't behave as a Frenchman does...

This French cultural hegemony has passed away for nearly a century now – and this is not for the worse. Another one has taken its place: American culture.[10] And again, one sees the same process occurring: from inside that culture, it is hard to understand how and why people from different cultures should think and act differently. The way for instance race or feminist issues are grasped through movements such as *Black lives Matter* or *#Metoo* is basically American. It doesn't mean it's wrong: it is peculiar. But conversely, it doesn't mean other ways, other sensibilities, are wrong – they are just different.

I believe that, if anything should be concluded from our conversation about time, it is this: mutual differences enrich us. It is more important to disagree than to agree, since it makes you think and search. It makes you discover, at the end the day. Agreement doesn't do this; it just convinces you to believe you are basically right. I have been deeply happy when you agreed with what I had discovered or observed, since we were, at that time, in harmony, although coming from two different directions. But I have been equally satisfied when you disagreed, since I knew you weren't thinking I was therefore wrong or stupid. You were just wondering how I had come to this point. And it was the same for me.

This book was a journey we made together across archaeological time. It has changed us; we aren't the same people we were at the beginning. I believe it has made us more tolerant and patient, more thoughtful toward each other. I speak for both of us when I say that writing this book has been a great joy and we are quite sad to put down these last lines and go our separate ways again. But first and last, we thank you, our readers, for providing us with this wonderful opportunity to make such a journey in your company.

Notes

1. C. Gamble, 'The Anthropology of Deep History', *Journal of the Royal Anthropological Institute* (N.S), 21 (2014): 147–64; also see, A. Shryock and D.L. Smail (eds), *Deep History: The Architecture of Past and Present* (Berkeley: University of California Press, 2011); A. Whittle, *The Times of Their Lives: Hunting History in the Archaeology of Neolithic Europe* (Oxford: Oxbow Books, 2017).
2. T. Kuhn, *The Structure of Scientific Revolutions* (University of Chicago Press, 1962).
3. F. Braudel, 'La longue durée', *Annales, Économies, Sociétés, Civilisations*, 13, no. 4 (1958): 725–753; C. Ginzburg, J. and A. Tedeschi, 'Microhistory: Two or Three Things That I know about It', *Critical Inquiry*, 20, no. 1 (1993): 10–35.
4. C. Ginzburg, *The Cheese and the Worms. The Cosmos of a Sixteenth-Century Miller* (Translated by John and Anne Tedeschi. London, Routledge and Kegan, 1980).
5. See for example, J. Robb and T. Pauketat (eds), *Big Histories, Human Lives: Tackling Problems of Scale in Archaeology* (Santa Fe: School of Advanced Research, 2013).
6. M. Foucault, *The Order of Things: an archaeology of the human sciences.* (New York: Vintage, 1973)
7. Parker Pearson, M. et al. 2021. 'The original Stonehenge? A dismantled stone circle in the Preseli Hills of west Wales'. *Antiquity* 95, no. 379 (2021): 85–103.
8. L. Olivier, 'How Celts perceived the world. Early Celtic Art and analogical thought', in Nimura, C., Chittock, H., Hommel, P., and Gosden C. (eds.), *Art in the Eurasian Iron Age. Context, Connections and Scale* (Oxford & Philadelphia: Oxbow Books, 2020), 95–109; L. Olivier, 'In the eye of the dragon: how the ancient Celts viewed the world', in Martin Toby, M. and Morrison W. (eds.), *Barbaric Splendour. The Use of Image Before and After Rome* (Oxford: Archaeopress, 2020), 18–33.
9. C.-C. Baudelot de Dairval, *Descriptions des bas-reliefs anciens trouvez depuis peu dans l'église cathédrale de Paris* (Paris: Pierre Cot, 1711).
10. L. Tournès, *Américanisation. Une histoire mondiale (XVIIIe-XXIe siècles)* (Paris: Fayard, L'épreuve de l'Histoire, 2020).

Bibliography

Baudelot de Dairval, C-C. *Descriptions des bas-reliefs anciens trouvez depuis peu dans l'église cathédrale de Pari`*, Paris: Pierre Cot, 1711.

Braudel, F. 'La longue durée', *Annales, Économies, Sociétés, Civilisations*, 13, no.4 (1958): 725–753.

Foucault, M. *The Order of Things: An Archaeology of the Human Sciences.* New York: Vintage, 1973.

Gamble, C. 'The Anthropology of Deep History', *Journal of the Royal Anthropological Institute* (N.S), 21 (2014): 147–164.

Ginzburg, C. *The Cheese and the Worms. The Cosmos of a Sixteenth-Century Miller.* Translated by John and Anne Tedeschi. London: Routledge and Kegan, 1980.

Ginzburg, C., J. Tedeschi and A. Tedeschi 'Microhistory: Two or Three Things That I know about It', *Critical Inquiry*, 20, no.1 (1993): 10–35.

Kuhn, T. *The Structure of Scientific Revolutions.* University of Chicago Press, 1962.

Olivier, L. 'How Celts perceived the world. Early Celtic Art and analogical thought', in Nimura, C., Chittock, H., Hommel, P., and Gosden C. (eds.), *Art in the Eurasian Iron Age. Context, Connections and Scale.* Oxford & Philadelphia: Oxbow Books, 2020, 95–109.

Olivier, L. 'In the eye of the dragon: how the ancient Celts viewed the world', in Martin Toby, M. and Morrison W. (eds.), *Barbaric Splendour. The use of image before and after Rome.* Oxford: Archaeopress, 2020, 18–33.

Parker Pearson, M. et al. 'The original Stonehenge? A dismantled stone circle in the Preseli Hills of west Wales'. *Antiquity* 95, no. 379 (2021): 85–103.

Robb J. and T. Pauketat (eds.). *Big Histories, Human Lives: Tackling Problems of Scale in Archaeology*, Santa Fe: School of Advanced Research, 2013.

Shryock A. and D.L. Smail (eds). *Deep History: The Architecture of Past and Present.* Berkeley: University of California Press, 2011.

Tournès L. *Américanisation. Une histoire mondiale (XVIIIe-XXIe siècles).* Paris: Fayard, L'épreuve de l'Histoire, 2020.

Whittle, A. *The Times of their Lives: Hunting History in the Archaeology of Neolithic Europe.* Oxford: Oxbow Books, 2017.

Epilogue

The conversation presented in the pages of this book took place over three months. It is a record of two archaeologists who knew each other's work well, yet still felt compelled to reach a closer understanding. As should be abundantly clear after having read this conversation, we constantly circle around an issue, sometimes getting very close and sharing the same views, only to separate again. As Laurent put it, we are like two planets in orbit, sometimes our paths converge, at other times we are on opposite sides. So what is it that we both seem to agree upon and where do we differ?

Many of the differences derive simply from our personal and cultural intellectual backgrounds. For Laurent, Freud on memory and the unconscious as well as the work of Walter Benjamin on Paris and the Arcades Project have provided fruitful ways to explore time in archaeology, while for Gavin, philosophy is almost always the first port of call, although in some ways he is also like a magpie, picking up anything that looks useful. Indeed, this may reflect a broader cultural difference between anglophone and francophone methods of scholarship. For Gavin, philosophy became a way to see archaeological problems that he could not see before; it helped to generate questions and problems. In contrast, for Laurent it is always the archaeology that first shows us the problems, while the philosophy comes later as a way to help move things along. Yet in some ways, these different ways of working often acted to obscure underlying commonalities as our conversation shows. Indeed, if we focus primarily on the matters of concern – the nature of time and archaeology – then ultimately, we feel there is more agreement than disagreement. Three issues in particular stand out: the distinctiveness of archaeological time; the relation between the past and the present; and the nature of past time.

1. The distinctiveness of archaeological time

Time as it is manifest in archaeological remains has a rather special character. Whereas our common, everyday sense of time is that of a relentlessly forward-moving flow from past to future, a time which passes, archaeological or material time has different speed settings, can stop, erase, reverse or fast forward. Archaeological objects are selective agglomerations of multiple times, they incorporate various and disparate traces of past events, but they exclude or erase such events as much as they preserve them. The archaeological record is this hybrid of preservation and transformation captured by the neologism 'transformission'. Archaeological time is the time made by things.
On this matter, we are in complete agreement.

2. The past only exists in the present

As a material presence, the past only exists in the present – *whenever* we might choose to situate that present. Archaeology therefore always has to approach the past as a trace in the present. An archaeology of the present (as distinct from the archaeology of the contemporary past) is a critical reflection on this condition and what it means for our interpretation of archaeological remains. It is both a methodological and theoretical exercise which requires that we look at how the persistence of the past in the present affects the stories we tell. Although it has some overlap with source criticism and formation theory, it is not reducible to these fields, but occupies a rather more open, less systematic space and one moreover, focused primarily on time and temporality.

On this issue, we are more or less in complete agreement again. The differences between us here largely relate to our distinct backgrounds and especially our different conceptions of theory; where Gavin would see an archaeology of the present as part of a wider tradition of source criticism and middle-range theory, Laurent views it as a more distinct and unique critique.

3. The nature of past time

The third and final issue is also the least developed as it concerns the nature of past time. It is also a corollary of the previous point. History as an extended flow of events is always a narrative construct after the fact; it has no actuality. History or more accurately *historicity* – the actuality of history – is not real; only the present is real which is usually experienced as a relatively short duration. This does not mean the past was not actual – but the past also only ever exists as a 'once-present' too. History is a fiction, a construction based on stitching together multiple past-presents into an extended present. In other words, 'history' (including archaeology) is grounded on temporality, not historicity.

On this issue, we both agree though its implications are even more hazy than the last. Moreover, where we perhaps differ is the implications this has for how we do archaeology, particularly the kind of narratives and stories we write and their relation to history. Where Gavin does not view the rejection of historicity *as necessarily leading to a rejection of archaeology as* history, *Laurent is drawn to the idea of an archaeology very different to history. However, the differences here are perhaps more one of degree than kind and possibly even solely terminological.*

This last point is, in many ways also the most important as it pertains to the wider goals and ambitions of archaeology. What is it that we are trying to do? In the spirit of co-operation, let us end this book with a joint proposal, a provocation for what archaeology does.

Three theses on archaeology

Thesis 1. We can never go back. Only forward

Since the past only exists in the present, and the present is always changing, the past will also always change too. To be clear though; we are not arguing that the past will always be *re-interpreted* differently by different generations. This is not a gloss on postmodernism. This may be the case, but that is not our point. Our argument concerns the materiality of the past-in-the-present, not its meaning; the persistence of the past within the present is always subtly transforming. This is about *Nachleben,* the *après-coup* or 'post-history' – the posthumous afterlives of things as they are entangled in later presents. The impact of the spatial layout of a Roman town creates one effect on its medieval successor, quite another on the same city in the 21st century; Roman urbanism is filtered through later centuries of medieval and postmedieval urbanism and at each moment, the character of that Roman past is altered, because it intersects with a different present. Each present makes its own past visible – but also renders others, invisible. A Neolithic pit cluster lying inert and forgotten beneath a farmer's field for thousands of years, only irrupting into the present by archaeologists as that field is converted into a housing development, reveals the importance of this dual process. Pasts are always filtered through the present.

Thesis 2. *Archaeology makes time*

From another perspective though, the past is not so much altered as a new past is created or more precisely, a new past-in-the-present. This is why the past is always also capable of bringing novelty into the world. Archaeology then becomes a practice devoted to cultivating this novelty from the past in our present; it keeps the past alive. Which brings us to the importance of archaeological stories; although not the only means of performing this act, stories remain one of the most powerful ways in which we keep this past alive. We re-presence the past, but not as a historicity, but as a work closer to fiction, a history or memory crafted by transforming the past-in-the-present into a presence-in-the-past but always preserving the tension between these two terms. None of our terms are quite adequate to capture this act of fiction; stories, history, memory – it is all of these but each also is burdened with prior discourses. We use the term fiction here not in the sense of its opposition to truth but in the sense of moulding, shaping, inventing this past-in-the-present relation.

Thesis 3. *Time is a relation*

If archaeology makes time, time is similarly not something that pre-exists things; things don't exist in time, rather time is emergent from things. Time is not a field or container, whether it comes pre-packaged into envelopes like periods, or a continuum divisible into moments like dates; this is time reduced to a metrology. Rather we see time as a relation, an aspect of the inter-action between things which both emerges from and defines them. Moreover, archaeology needs to recover a sense of things in motion, in flux, of time as a dynamic and constitutive relation; the time that is emergent from things is active. Time is a verb, not a noun. If archaeology is a discipline defined, in part, by temporality, then this is not because it deals with things in time, but rather because it deals with the timing of things, of the temporal relations, agencies, interactions that together, weave the world.

Index

For Product Safety Concerns and Information please contact our EU
representative GPSR@taylorandfrancis.com
Taylor & Francis Verlag GmbH, Kaufingerstraße 24, 80331 München, Germany

www.ingramcontent.com/pod-product-compliance
Lightning Source LLC
Chambersburg PA
CBHW050535270326
41926CB00015B/3235